James Dean

These and other titles are included in The Importance Of biography series:

Alexander the Great	Harry Houdini
Muhammad Ali	Thomas Jefferson
Maya Angelou	Mother Jones
Louis Armstrong	Chief Joseph
James Baldwin	John F. Kennedy
Clara Barton	Martin Luther King Jr.
The Beatles	Joe Louis
Alexander Graham Bell	Douglas MacArthur
Napoleon Bonaparte	Malcolm X
Julius Caesar	Thurgood Marshall
Rachel Carson	Margaret Mead
Charlie Chaplin	Golda Meir
Charlemagne	Michelangelo
Cesar Chavez	Wolfgang Amadeus
Winston Churchill	Mozart
Cleopatra	John Muir
Christopher Columbus	Sir Isaac Newton
Hernando Cortes	Richard M. Nixon
Marie Curie	Georgia O'Keeffe
Charles Dickens	Louis Pasteur
Emily Dickinson	Pablo Picasso
Walt Disney	Elvis Presley
Amelia Earhart	Jackie Robinson
Thomas Edison	Norman Rockwell
Albert Einstein	Eleanor Roosevelt
Duke Ellington	Anwar Sadat
F. Scott Fitzgerald	Margaret Sanger
Dian Fossey	Oskar Schindler
Anne Frank	William Shakespeare
Benjamin Franklin	John Steinbeck
Galileo Galilei	Tecumseh
Emma Goldman	Mother Teresa
Jane Goodall	Jim Thorpe
Martha Graham	Mark Twain
Lorraine Hansberry	Queen Victoria
Stephen Hawking	Pancho Villa
Ernest Hemingway	Leonardo da Vinci
Jim Henson	H. G. Wells
Adolf Hitler	Simon Weisenthal

THE IMPORTANCE OF

James Dean

by Walter Oleksy

Lucent Books, P.O. Box 289011, San Diego, CA 92198-9011

Library of Congress Cataloging-in-Publication Data

Oleksy, Walter G., 1930–
    James Dean / by Walter Oleksy.
        p. cm.—(The importance of)
    Includes bibliographical references and index.
    Summary: Examines the life and accomplishments of film
actor James Dean including his life as an orphan with a father
and as a troubled young loner, his experiments with acting
and life, his success, his roles as a movie teen rebel, and his
death.
    ISBN 1-56006-698-9 (alk. paper)
    1. Dean, James, 1931–1955—Juvenile literature. 2. Motion
picture actors and actresses—United States—Biography—
Juvenile literature. [1. Dean, James, 1931–1955. 2. Actors and
actresses.] I. Title. II. Series.
    PN2287.D33 O44 2001
    791.43'028'092—dc21
                                                      00-009236

Contents

Foreword

THE IMPORTANCE OF biography series deals with individuals who have made a unique contribution to history. The editors of the series have deliberately chosen to cast a wide net and include people from all fields of endeavor. Individuals from politics, music, art, literature, philosophy, science, sports, and religion are all represented. In addition, the editors did not restrict the series to individuals whose accomplishments have helped change the course of history. Of necessity, this criterion would have eliminated many whose contribution was great, though limited. Charles Darwin, for example, was responsible for radically altering the scientific view of the natural history of the world. His achievements continue to impact the study of science today. Others, such as Chief Joseph of the Nez Percé, played a pivotal role in the history of their own people. While Joseph's influence does not extend much beyond the Nez Percé, his nonviolent resistance to white expansion and his continuing role in protecting his tribe and his homeland remain an inspiration to all.

These biographies are more than factual chronicles. Each volume attempts to emphasize an individual's contributions both in his or her own time and for posterity. For example, the voyages of Christopher Columbus opened the way to European colonization of the New World. Unquestionably, his encounter with the New World brought monumental changes to both Europe and the Americas in his day. Today, however, the broader impact of Columbus's voyages is being critically scrutinized. *Christopher Columbus,* as well as every biography in The Importance Of series, includes and evaluates the most recent scholarship available on each subject.

Each author includes a wide variety of primary and secondary source quotations to document and substantiate his or her work. All quotes are footnoted to show readers exactly how and where biographers derive their information, as well as provide stepping stones to further research. These quotations enliven the text by giving readers eyewitness views of the life and times of each individual covered in The Importance Of series.

Finally, each volume is enhanced by photographs, bibliographies, chronologies, and comprehensive indexes. For both the casual reader and the student engaged in research, The Importance Of biographies will be a fascinating adventure into the lives of people who have helped shape humanity's past and present, and who will continue to shape its future.

IMPORTANT DATES IN THE LIFE OF JAMES DEAN

1931
James Dean is born February 8, in Marion, Indiana.

1940
Mildred Dean dies of cancer on April 14; Jimmy begins living with relatives on a farm near Fairmount, Indiana.

1949
Graduates from high school on May 16 and moves to California on June 15.

1930   1935   1940   1945   1950

1936
Moves with parents to Santa Monica, California.

1950
Briefly attends Santa Monica City College in January; transfers to the University of California at Los Angeles in the fall; appears in television commercial.

1955

Stars in *Rebel Without a Cause*; becomes a leading new young actor when *East of Eden* is released; stars in *Giant*; finishes filming *Giant* on September 22; is killed in auto accident on September 30 near Cholame, California; begins to become international teenage cult figure when *Rebel* is released to theaters.

1956

Giant is released to theaters and wins more acclaim for Dean.

1951

Leaves college for acting career; appears in minor roles in three movies. Moves to New York City.

1952	1953	1954	1955	1956

1953

Appears in numerous television dramas.

1954

Appears in *The Immoralist* on Broadway; arrives in Hollywood on March 8 to star in *East of Eden*; falls in love with Pier Angeli but loses her to Vic Damone.

1952

Briefly becomes member of Actors Studio; appears on television and in plays on and off Broadway.

1956–present

James Dean cult continues.

Rebel with a Cause

Appearing in just three movies made within eighteen months before his death in an auto crash at the age of twenty-four in 1955, James Dean came to personify troubled, rebellious youth. A worldwide James Dean "cult" began after his death and survives to the present time. Each new generation of teenagers relates to his enigmatic life as a loner and his movie portrayals of alienated youth.

Dean's life and death had far-reaching social effects on his generation and those that have come since. Sal Mineo, who ap-peared with Dean in his last two films, said, "Jimmy Dean started the youth movement of the 1950s. He was the first rebel. The first to ask the questions . . . why? He was the first to give teenagers any identification of any kind."[1]

During the 1950s and 1960s Dean's fame spread around the world. By the 1980s he had become one of a handful of American popular cultural figures. Some people built shrines in their homes to Dean. Others identified with him to the point that they imitated him in dress, stance, and voice.

Sal Mineo (left) and James Dean in a scene from Rebel Without a Cause. *Dean's portrayal of a rebellious, troubled youth made him an idol for teenagers around the world.*

Although to his fans, James Dean became a symbol of unfocused rebellion, in truth, Dean was a rebel with at least three obsessions. He wanted to become the best actor in Hollywood and the best race car driver in the world. But his main cause, or quest, was to find himself—to settle uncertainties about his sexual orientation, his relationship with his father, and his relationships with his fellow actors and actresses.

James Dean was a complex, enigmatic person, both as an actor and as a human being. Following his death, no one, not even his relatives or the few close friends he had made, claimed to have understood him. In part this was because they believed Dean fantasized about his life as a boy and teenager, leaving those around him uncertain whether they were hearing the truth or a concoction of half-truths and outright falsehoods.

Dean was a charismatic but flawed human, unable to put his unhappy childhood behind him and get on with life. He was aware of his faults, but he was either not able to or did not live long enough to reckon with them. A psychiatrist who treated Dean just a few months before his death has stated that deep-rooted emotional problems stemming from Dean's childhood caused him to suffer from a personality disorder.

While flawed as a person, Dean the actor was something finer. The famous artist Andy Warhol once said of Dean, "James Dean's not our hero because he was perfect, but because he perfectly represented the damaged but beautiful soul of our time."[2]

Young people who see his movies today and in the future may recognize themselves, especially in *Rebel Without a Cause*. The movie remains James Dean's legacy to teens everywhere, in every generation, as does his unhappy and tragic life story.

1 Orphan with a Father

As a young boy, James Dean felt deeply loved by his mother, but he did not feel loved by his father, whom he seemed unable to please. His mother's death when he was nine and his father's decision to send him to live with relatives on a farm in Indiana, left Jimmy emotionally scarred, feeling unwanted and alone in the world.

As a young child, James Dean had a delicate constitution despite his sturdy appearance.

A Doting Mother and a Distant Father

James Dean was born on February 8, 1931, in the small industrial town of Marion, Indiana, about forty miles north of Indianapolis.

Jimmy's father, Winton Dean, age twenty-two, was a slim, handsome, quiet man with blond hair and blue eyes, a farmer's son who worked as a dental technician at the local veterans hospital. Jimmy's mother, nineteen-year-old Mildred Wilson Dean was a shy, plump, dark-haired farm girl who worked as a clerk in a drugstore.

Mildred Dean gave birth in the couple's rented apartment in a two-story wood-frame building at Fourth and McClure Streets. They named their son James Byron, after a friend of Winton's who also was the attending physician, James Emmick, and for Mildred's favorite poet, Lord Byron. Mildred's pet name for her son was "Deanie," but his father and others called him Jimmy.

Mildred was by all accounts a doting mother. She had been raised with an appreciation of the arts and culture, so she exposed her son to these interests. As he grew older, she gave Jimmy crayons

The infant James Dean at play in the family garden.

to draw with and read him stories and poetry.

When Jimmy was only three years old, his mother enrolled him in a tap dance class at the Marion College of Dance and Theatrical Arts, and there he proved to be a capable dancer. Zina Gladys Pitsor, owner of the dance school, later recalled a recital young Jimmy was in: "Jimmy did an intricate tap dance routine, and his cousin Joan Winslow did a waltz clog. Joan was older and very talented, but little Jimmy upstaged her with his bright smile and quick legs. The audience loved him."[3]

Jimmy's artistic abilities pleased his mother, but not his father. Winton con-sidered art and dancing unmasculine and therefore not proper pastimes for a boy. Mildred's closeness to Jimmy and her urging his involvement in the arts es-tranged Winton from his son.

Jimmy engaged in dancing and artistic endeavors, but he was not a healthy child. Although he was sturdy-looking in build, he was delicate by constitution, often suf-fering from nosebleeds, sinus problems, and internal bleeding that caused black and blue marks on his arms and legs.

His grandmother, Emma Dean, said, "He was a sweet-looking child with fea-tures of a china doll. Almost too dainty for a boy."[4]

A New Life in California

Jimmy's life changed dramatically when he was five. The nation was in the midst of the Great Depression, a decade-long period of unemployment and poverty for millions of people. In spite of the hard times, the Deans lived a middle-class life in Marion until Winton was laid off at the veterans hospital. Then Winton learned of a job for a dental technician at the Sawtelle Veterans Hospital in Santa Monica, California. He suggested to Mildred that he go to California alone first; if he got the job and thought they would be better off relocating there, he would come back for her and Jimmy.

Mildred was delighted with the prospect of living in California. She was not particularly fond of Marion, where she had grown up and lived all her life. She had always wanted to travel, and she saw this move as her big chance to see more of the world. Besides, she thought California's climate would be good for Jimmy's health.

At Mildred's pleading, Winton agreed to take his family with him right away. The Deans made the trip by train as a family in June 1936. Winton got the dental technician's job, and they were living in a small rented bungalow in Santa Monica, just two miles from the beach.

During Jimmy's first year in California, his mother tutored him in the arts at home. Besides encouraging him to draw, she bought him a child-sized violin and enrolled him in lessons.

James Dean's Mother

Mildred Dean was a complex, enigmatic woman, according to one of James Dean's few close friends, John Gilmore, an actor-director-screenwriter, who described her in his book Live Fast—Die Young: Remembering the Short Life of James Dean.

"Mystery has always clouded Jimmy's mother; she seems to have left little of herself in the world, most of it invested into Jimmy's memories. But from what is known, she emerges as a sensitive person believing herself to be out of place—as though born in some other time and place and abandoned on a farm in Indiana. . . .

[Jimmy would] spend the remainder of his life searching out substitutes for the acceptance—apart from his mother's—that he never received as a child. . . .

[Winton Dean had told his own mother that] Jimmy and [Mildred] had been 'too close—abnormally close.' While he'd tried to get close to the boy, too many problems between Winton and Mildred had stood in the way."

SCHOOL DAYS

In 1937, when Jimmy was six, he entered kindergarten at McKinley Elementary School. He did not adjust readily to school, a fact that his teachers noticed early on. One teacher later recalled, "The impression he gave was that he thought he was being punished by having to attend school. When told there were many things to learn in school, he said he could learn more at home than he could be taught at school."[5]

School was not a pleasant experience for Jimmy in other ways as well. He was very sensitive, and when criticized, he would begin to cry. Making friends was also hard for him.

Seeing that her son did not mix well with other children at school, Mildred began spending more time with him at home and indulged his every whim. He would draw pictures of things he wanted to do or have, then put them under his pillow, and Mildred provided as best she could. Winton then thought Jimmy spent far too much time with his mother and too little time with boys and girls his own age.

Mildred also encouraged Jimmy's artistic inclinations. When Jimmy showed an interest in drama, Mildred built him a toy theater constructed of an upturned cardboard box pinned with curtains. The front porch served as an imaginary stage for their theater as mother and son acted out stories with puppets and dolls. Again, Winton did not approve. To him, playacting with puppets and dolls was not a masculine activity and was therefore in-

Jimmy had a difficult time adjusting to school and making friends with other children.

appropriate for a boy. Winton often complained to Mildred that Jimmy seemed girlish at times.

FATHER AND SON

Jimmy and his father were often at odds in other ways. Winton regarded his son as a strong-willed, even obstinate child. "You'd try to order him to do or not to do something and he'd just sit there with his little face all screwed up and closed," Winton later recalled. "It didn't take you very long to realize that you weren't going to get anywhere with him. Spankings didn't help. Scolding didn't. And you couldn't bribe him."[6]

A Mother's Love

"If criticized, Jimmy was easily brought to tears. He told his mother that some children who had done something wrong [at school] were taken to the office, where they were spanked with a big paddle. It was called 'getting swats,' one teacher said to him, and for weeks Jimmy seemed anxious that such a fate was going to happen to him. . . .

At home he tried to tell his mother of his fears and she'd try to distract him by having him practice the violin. More stories would be read, with Mildred energetically acting out the characters until Jimmy'd giggle. When they'd laugh together his tears would be gone."

As a child, James Dean felt closer to his mother than he did to his father.

A big part of the inability of father and son to connect was Winton's disapproval of Jimmy's artistic endeavors. As John Gilmore, one of Jimmy's few friends in later years, explained,

Winton frequently complained that Jimmy seemed "girlish" at times. No "red-blooded boy" should be satisfied to spend more time with his mother than with playmates his own age.

Later in life, depending on who was around, Jimmy would boast about the closeness he shared with his father. But he was never able to keep the truth from himself. Because Winton was unable to show enthusiasm for the violin lessons, or the tap dancing, or the poetry his mother read or the stories she'd tell him, Jimmy withdrew from his father; who, though aware of the distance between them, made little or no effort to close it. And with the increasing coolness between Winton and Mildred, for Jimmy the differences were to prove irreconcilable.[7]

However, Winton did make some effort to close the gap between himself and his son. To encourage Jimmy to engage in what he considered more masculine pursuits, Winton tried to interest him in sports. His efforts to teach Jimmy baseball were at first disastrous. Jimmy failed at both batting and catching. His poor skills led to the discovery that his clumsiness was the result of poor eyesight. Severely nearsighted, he was fitted for eyeglasses, which he wore the rest of his life. Aided by glasses, Jimmy began batting and catching more effectively. He also showed an interest in basketball for the first time.

Yet, despite some interest and aptitude for sports, Jimmy still did not feel as close to his father as he did to his mother. He felt unable to understand his father. Years later he said,

> I never understood what he was after, what sort of person he'd been, because he never tried to get on my side of the fence, or to try and see things the way I saw them when I was little. I was always with my mother and we were very close.[8]

Winton Dean's alienation from his son was described years later by John Gilmore, in whom Jimmy sometimes confided about his boyhood years. As Gilmore writes in a biography of James Dean,

> Aside from going to school, most of [Jimmy's] time was spent being protected by his mother; looking forward to music lessons, and to having poems

[she wrote] read to him—a behavior that caused his father to believe that his son had unmanly tendencies, was not a normal boy, and Winton would soon separate himself from his son.[9]

Gilmore and others who knew Jimmy later recalled that he indulged in wishful thinking about his relationship with his father. He was often suspected of making up a happier father-son relationship than there actually had been. Gilmore recalled, "When Jimmy was older, he would make great pretenses to others about the closeness and the warmth he shared with his distant father."[10]

A DEATH IN THE FAMILY

Although Jimmy had begun to make a few friends and adjust to life in California, his mother was disappointed by the move

Young Jimmy often felt that he did not understand his father.

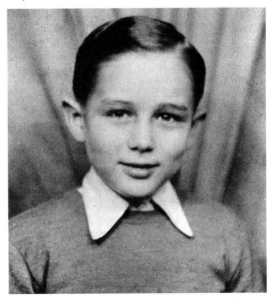

she had made. She told a friend visiting from Indiana in 1938, "I don't want Jimmy to grow up out here. I've even been thinking about going back home to Indiana. Everything's so artificial here. I want my Jimmy to grow up where things are real and simple."[11]

But before Mildred could do anything about moving back to Indiana, she became ill. When Jimmy was eight, she underwent surgery that revealed that she had breast cancer, and her health deteriorated over the next year. As his wife weakened, Winton sent train fare for his mother, Emma Dean, to come to Santa Monica and help care for Mildred.

While Winton could see that Mildred was dying, he also could tell from Jimmy's casual attitude when he was at his mother's bedside, that his son refused to accept the fact. Winton explained years later,

> I tried to get it across to him, to prepare him in some way, but he just couldn't seem to take it in. I told him straight out one evening [while Mildred was in the hospital], "Your mother's never coming home again." All he did was stare at me! [12]

Mildred Dean died on April 14, 1940, when Jimmy was nine. When his father told him the news, Jimmy sat blankly, his eyes, without tears, fixed and distant. His mother's death, however, was only the first of two emotional traumas.

A SECOND BLOW

Mildred's long illness had so depleted the family's finances that Winton had to sell his car to meet expenses. Seeing how difficult it would be for him to raise Jimmy alone under strained finances and as a single parent, Winton's mother suggested that he send Jimmy back to Indiana to be raised by Winton's sister and brother-in-law, Ortense and Marcus Winslow, on their farm near the town of Fairmount. She told him, "Now Winton, I want you to think this over carefully. If you see fit to let Jimmy come back to Fairmount, Ortense and Marcus would like to take him. They'll raise him for you, if you want."[13] Winton sat and thought about the idea. After a few moments, he accepted his mother's suggestion.

Some members of the family criticized Winton for his decision, saying that he was, in effect, abandoning his son.

Years later, Winton explained why he sent his son to live with relatives: "You can't find a finer man than Marcus Winslow, and so far as choosing between the way my sister would mother Jimmy and how some housekeeper would take care of him, there's just no question."[14]

The choice was not an easy one to make since another option was available. Mildred's sister, Ruth Stegmoller, who had moved from Indiana to Los Angeles when Mildred became ill, volunteered to help rear her nephew. "I told Winton that I would stay out there and take care of Jimmy," she told an interviewer years later. "I would have done it for the sake of Jimmy. But Winton and his mother had talked it over and that was the decision they wanted to make."[15]

Jimmy did not understand his father's reason for sending him away, and doubts about it troubled him. Years later Jimmy would recall that when his father told him of the plan to send him to Indiana to live with relatives, he felt abandoned. In this recollection, he admitted that as a boy, because he had been unable to please his father, he had suspected that his father did not love or want him.

Emma Dean accompanied her grandson on the sad journey back to Indiana. Unable to afford round-trip train fare for himself so he could accompany them and attend his wife's funeral, Winton Dean stayed behind in California. Six days after he left California, Jimmy stood silent and dazed at the graveside service for his mother at Grant Memorial Park Cemetery in Marion, her hometown.

The grief Jimmy felt was sharp at first. Several times during the following months he rode his bicycle from his aunt and uncle's farm on the outskirts of Fairmount to Marion, ten miles away, to visit his mother's grave.

Some who knew Jimmy believe that he never reconciled himself to his mother's death or to his father's decision to send him to live with relatives. Marietta Cantry, an actress who later worked with Dean, said he once confided to her his belief that God could not possibly care about him because "just look at the dirty trick He played on me with my mother and father."[16]

Chapter

2 A Troubled Young Loner

Confused and troubled, Jimmy faced a difficult time in the next few years in Indiana. He was unable to feel a part of his aunt and uncle's family, and he withdrew into himself at home and at school. Jimmy grew into his teen years as a troubled—and somewhat troublesome—loner. Neither adults nor his peers felt they understood or could get close to him, except a minister who became his mentor. As he sought to come to terms with the loss of his mother and with his distant father, he began to find a world he felt he

belonged in, and a possible future for himself, in acting.

JIMMY THE FARM BOY

Jimmy reluctantly settled into his new home on his aunt and uncle's farm in Indiana. Ortense and Marcus Winslow reared him as if he were their own son. They already had a daughter, Joan, who was fourteen when nine-year-old Jimmy came to live with them.

Following his mother's death, James Dean was sent to live on his aunt and uncle's farm.

How Others Saw Young Jimmy Dean

Jimmy's speech and drama teacher, Adeline Brookshire Nall, said his grades were good, but that he could have been an even better scholar had he not consciously sabotaged his own academic performance.

Donald Spoto quotes Nall in his book Rebel, The Life and Legend of James Dean:

"He had a bright mind — but didn't always apply himself. He used to say, 'I'd rather not get good grades than be called a sissy.'"

Jimmy's classmates regarded him as being somewhat different than they were. "We watched Jimmy with a little awe, but felt he was explosive and not part of the community," Sue Hill says in Val Holley's book *James Dean: The Biography*. "We were aware he marched to a different drummer than ninety-nine percent of Fairmount."

Despite their efforts to make him feel a part of the family, Jimmy never felt a real closeness to the Winslows, nor did he come to like life on the farm. His uncle worked the farm without hired help, so Jimmy was expected to pitch in. But he merely tolerated the daily chores such as milking cows, feeding chickens, and sweeping the barn. Years later he recalled that he treated this part of his life as someone might a theatrical role: "[It] was a real farm, and I worked like crazy as long as someone was watching me. Forty acres of oats made a huge stage, and when the audience left I took a nap and nothing got plowed or harrowed."[17]

Despite his distaste for his farm life, Jimmy knew it was important to his aunt and uncle that he keep his true feelings to himself. Another time, also years later, he said, "I was never a farmer. I always wanted out of there, but I never ran away, because I never wanted to hurt anyone."[18]

For their part, the Winslows did not consider Jimmy to be a bad or destructive boy, just sometimes a bit mischievous. His aunt recalls that he did not always think twice about the consequences of his actions. For example, once, while Jimmy was in a field of dry grass on the farm, he playfully struck some matches. The grass caught fire and a large section of field went up in flames. The Fairmount Fire Department sped to the farm and put out the blaze.

Elementary School

Attending elementary school in nearby Fairmount, Jimmy was a good pupil, but he was quieter than most of the other boys and girls. He became regarded as a loner by classmates. They considered him to be an outsider since he was the new boy in town.

His teachers noticed that Jimmy was often melancholy. "He was sometimes moody, and often unexpectedly stubborn," recalled one of his teachers, India Nose. "He could be forgetful, too, as if he were lost in a daze. Sudden noises would startle him and questions in class seemed to interrupt some faraway thoughts."[19]

Still artistic and actively drawing, painting, and by then molding clay, Jimmy found acting to be another major interest. Even before he reached his teens, he began to appear in plays at the Back Creek Friends Church, which he attended with the Winslows on Sundays.

EXCELLING IN SPORTS

Jimmy's reputation as a loner followed him as he grew. When he enrolled as a freshman at Fairmount High School, he did not mix in well with the other boys and girls and rarely spoke to them.

Despite his tendency to keep to himself, sports became an outlet for Jimmy. Sports were both a way to challenge the athletic abilities that he knew he possessed, and to prove that he was masculine. "I felt a need to prove myself,"[20] he recalled about this time.

Despite his yearning to excel at sports, Jimmy needed help if he was to try out for his school's basketball team. His Uncle Marcus, who once had ambitions of being an athletic coach, taught Jimmy to dribble, pass, and shoot.

Armed with the skills his uncle taught him, Jimmy tried out for the basketball team, even though he was not as tall as the other boys. He stood about five feet, seven inches tall and weighed 140 pounds. He later said that as a teenager, he considered himself to be "runty."[21]

Even though he was smaller than most basketball players, Jimmy became a guard on his school's basketball team. Soon his teammates began to notice the small player with the eyeglasses who had to jump high to sink baskets. They began calling him "Jumping Jim."

To show he could outplay the other boys, Jimmy leaped higher and crashed into opponents recklessly as he scrambled to catch rebounds or fired the ball at the

In high school, Jimmy's aggressive style of play helped him become an outstanding basketball player.

An aggressive and temperamental athlete, Jimmy (front row, center), participated in many sports, including baseball.

basket. Thanks to his aggressive style of play, Jimmy became a top scorer. He averaged eight points per game (an impressive record for high school basketball players at the time), mainly by his skill at sinking long shots.

And basketball was not the only sport that Jimmy tried out for. He also became a relief pitcher on the baseball diamond and a very determined hurdler on the track team. No matter what sport he played, he proved to be both an aggressive and temperamental athlete.

Jimmy's classmates also thought he seemed to be in competition with everyone about everything. One fellow student, Sue Hill, later recalled, "You got the sense that he would push as far as he could with someone, not just in basketball with the referees but in everything with everyone."[22]

While Jimmy became more accepted in school because of his athletic prowess, he remained distant on a personal level and continued to be regarded by his classmates as a loner. Also, sports were not his main interest, as he wrote years later in a journal he kept: "[Athletics is] the heartbeat of every American boy, [but] I think my life will be dedicated to art and dramatics."[23]

A DISCOVERY

Sports were one outlet for Jimmy's aggression and frustration, but soon he discovered another. For his sixteenth birthday, Jimmy's aunt and uncle gave him a one-and-a-half horsepower motorbike called a "Whizzer" that was capable of speeds as high as fifty miles an hour. The little engine could be heard a mile away as Jimmy sped over the countryside.

DEAN ON DEAN

James Dean wrote an autobiographical essay that Roland DuBois, the principal, had assigned to all students at Fairmount High School. Dean's description of his early years are quoted by Paul Alexander in his book Boulevard of Broken Dreams: The Life, Times, and Legend of James Dean:

"I had always lived such a talented life. I studied violin, played in concerts, tapdanced on theater stages but most of all I like art, to mount and create things with my hands.

I came back to Indiana to live with my uncle. I lost the dancing and violin, but not the art. I think my life will be devoted to art and dramatics. And there are so many different fields of art it would be hard to foul up. And if I did there are so many different things to do—farm, sports, science, geology, coaching, teaching, music. I got it, and I know that if I better myself there will be no match. A fellow must have confidence. . . .

As one strives to make a goal in a game there should be a goal in this crazy world for each of us. I hope I know where mine is, anyway, I'm after it. I don't mind telling you, Mr. DuBois, this is the hardest subject to write about considering the information one knows of himself, I ever attempted."

Jimmy also had fun at his schoolmates' expense by speeding in front of Fairmount High and making the other students leap out of his way. He would also take friends on rides, going so fast that they would plead with him to stop. His favorite daredevil stunt was to race along at fifty miles an hour while lying flat on the saddle.

At home on the farm, Jimmy revealed a darker side of his nature by taking pleasure in frightening the animals. "I used to go out for the cows on the motorcycle," Jimmy later recalled. "Scared the hell out of them. They'd get to running and their udders would start swinging and they'd lose a quart of milk."[24]

Jimmy's speeding on his motorbike also revealed what some later considered to be an early self-destructive side of his nature. A classmate, Dick Beck, who had ridden with Jimmy as a teenager, later recalled how Jimmy liked to court disaster by pushing his little motorbike to its limits by speeding toward an apple tree on a curve near Fairmount's Park Cemetery. It was an S curve on a gravel road that became known as Suicide Curve because of the many accidents that had occurred there. Beck recalled, "Jimmy would drive down the road flat-out toward the curve, and come so close to the tree that he could either reach out and touch it or kick it."[25]

Jimmy never owned a car while a teenager, but he loved to take his Uncle Marcus's old pickup truck for spins. As he did with his motorbike, Jimmy pushed the limits. Once, a boy challenged Jimmy to a race around Suicide Curve. Jimmy drove so fast that the other boy's car rolled over and crashed.

Some people thought Jimmy's motives for such recklessness were the same as for excelling in sports: to prove he was masculine. "[Jimmy] worked hard at being a basketball player to prove himself to those people in Fairmount," recalled Jack Raup, a longtime resident. "He rode a motorcycle because he had to prove he was a man."[26]

His aunt and uncle tolerated his antics with the motorbike and pickup truck, but they were disappointed that he was not more helpful on the farm. During his junior year in high school, Jimmy began to rebel against authority both at home and at school. "He became hard to handle, and we didn't know what was the matter," Marcus Winslow said years later. "He didn't take any more stock in us and refused to help out. We were at wits' end. He was no longer one of us."[27]

UNPOPULAR WITH GIRLS

Although he had the opportunity to date, Jimmy rarely did so during his high school years. The only exceptions were the occasional couples-only school dances to which boys were required to bring a girl.

While Jimmy rarely asked girls for dates, for their part, girls were cautious about Jimmy, as his classmate Sue Hill later recalled: "[He was] a little off-limits— almost juvenile delinquent status."[28]

Another classmate, Barbara Leach, later recalled that Jimmy also liked to play pranks. She said that at a Halloween party in a barn, "Dean hid up in the loft and tried to pour apple cider [on] the kids below."[29]

JIMMY THE ACTOR

As much as Jimmy Dean liked sports and racing his motorbike, what he loved most

As James Dean grew up, he began to rebel against authority, both at home and at school.

was acting. He practiced his acting skills partly by mimicking others. His Aunt Ortense recalled her nephew's behavior:

> If Grandpa Dean sat with his legs crossed, Jimmy crossed his. If Grandpa stretched his legs out, Jimmy did, too. It was more than just mocking Grandpa's gestures. Jimmy seemed able to be another person. His gift for make-believe had us helpless with laughter one moment and gripped the next moment by a sudden change of mood.[30]

In addition to enjoying mimicking people, Jimmy had the ability to project what he was feeling. His aunt later explained:

> [Jimmy had] a real talent for making you share his emotions. If he came home and was sad about something or someone had hurt him, it made you want to just go out and get whoever had made him unhappy. On the other hand, if he was in a good mood, you had to feel happy with him.[31]

James Dean displayed a unique talent as a mimic.

JIMMY THE LONER AND REBEL

Jimmy's basketball coach, Paul Weaver, noticed that Jimmy was a loner, according to Donald Spoto in *Rebel, The Life and Legend of James Dean*. "He was a little different from most boys," Weaver remembered. "He was usually alone, and when the team arrived [in the gym], usually kids came together. But Jimmy would usually arrive alone."

Weaver also said, "I felt sometimes that he had an inferiority complex that he was covering up. In any case, he wasn't too coachable and couldn't take criticism in front of others."

His drama teacher at Fairmount High, Adeline Brookshire Nall, recognized Jimmy's talent for acting and cast him in many school plays. By the time of his senior class play, Jimmy was cast as Grandpa Vanderhof in *You Can't Take It with You*, the George S. Kaufman and Moss Hart comedy. Nall thought that only Jimmy had the talent to play the cranky old man, a pivotal character in the play.

Like Jimmy's aunt, Nall also noticed that he was very observing of people and knew how to get their attention. "'It's better to be noticed than ignored,' he'd tell me," she recalled. "That's how he [later] got all that publicity in Hollywood, you see."[32]

Nall remembered her star student as someone who was both difficult and gifted:

> He could be moody and unpredictable, to keep people off their guard—and rude, to attract attention. One day, to shock everybody, he offered me a cigarette right in the middle of class. I almost popped him one for that.

> And if he didn't win a competition in something—oh, he could pout and rant like I don't know what.

> But I also recognized a natural talent. The boy had a gift—he knew it and I knew it. [33]

Jimmy's temperament was also apparent to the other drama students. A fellow cast member in school plays, Joyce John, later said Dean was often late for practice and sometimes did not show up at all. He had a temper and would walk out of practice if things did not suit him. "He was disruptive," she recalled. "But he was good!"[34]

Another trait that Nall recognized was the thin skin that Jimmy had demonstrated ever since elementary school. She said he could not take criticism, something he would demonstrate again a few years later when he became a stage and movie actor.

And there was something else, his drama teacher recalled. "Jim knew how to play people. He could work me around his little finger."[35]

Learning About Himself

In many ways, Jimmy wanted what everyone wants: to establish his own identity, to prove that he possessed some quality that set him apart, and to learn about life, especially beyond where he lived. During his junior year in high school, he sought the wisdom of a local minister, the Reverend James DeWeerd. In many ways, DeWeerd was to have a profound influence on the impressionable teenager.

To many of the boys of Fairmount, DeWeerd was someone to admire. The young pastor of Fairmount's Wesleyan church was a war hero, having been wounded twice during World War II. After rescuing injured soldiers in Italy, he had been awarded the Silver Star and the Purple Heart.

Jimmy enjoyed frequent visits to DeWeerd's house, where the minister played classical records, read poetry to him, and taught him how to relax with yoga. DeWeerd later recalled, "Jimmy was usually happiest stretched out on my library floor reading Shakespeare or other books of his choosing. He loved good music playing softly in the background; Tchaikovsky was his favorite."[36]

DeWeerd also encouraged Jimmy to try new things. "The more things you know how to do, and the more things you experience, the better off you will be,"[37] he told Jimmy. It was just what the lonely teenager, eager to learn what lay ahead in life, was eager to hear.

The pastor not only became Dean's only close friend in Fairmount, but he was likely the only person to whom Jimmy revealed his deepest feelings and innermost thoughts. DeWeerd later said that on one occasion, Jimmy confided his deepest secrets to him:

> Jimmy [said he believed] that he must be evil, or his mother would not have died and his father wouldn't have sent him away.
>
> He said he believed the ghost of his dead mother came to him. The dark scared him, he said, and he was afraid he'd suffocate as if being buried alive. When his mother "came" to him, the fear would be taken away.
>
> He seemed to be carrying some self-imposed responsibility for his mother's early death.[38]

Although such guilt was unwarranted, the pastor made use of it. Convinced that he could help Jimmy achieve a spiritual renewal, DeWeerd harnessed Jimmy's negative view of himself and the consequences of it. "I taught Jim that he was depraved and vile, that he had to seek salvation,"[39] DeWeerd said later.

DeWeerd later claimed in an interview that he had made a spiritual connection with Jimmy: "All of us are lonely and searching. But, because he was so sensitive, Jimmy was lonelier and he searched harder. He wanted final answers, and I think that I taught him to believe in personal immortality."[40] DeWeerd went on to say of Jimmy, "He had no fear of death because he believed, as I do, that death is merely a control of mind over matter."[41]

DeWeerd noticed something about Jimmy that others were also to see in his later years: He recognized a self-interested, opportunistic side to Dean, whom he called a "moocher." "[He] tried to get as much from you as possible. If he didn't consider you worth anything [to him], he dropped you."[42]

Similarly, DeWeerd also noticed what Dean's Aunt Ortense had: Jimmy's habit of mimicking others. Just as he had mimicked his grandfather's and other men's mannerisms, he also imitated the pastor's. This habit also was noticed by Al Yerhune, editor of the *Fairmount News*, who later said, "Jimmy was a parasitic type of person. He hung around DeWeerd a lot, picked up his mannerisms, and absorbed whatever he could."[43]

A NEW LIFE BECKONS

As Jimmy approached high school graduation, he began looking beyond the limited world of Fairmount and his life on the farm. It was at that point that his father came back into his life. Winton wrote to Jimmy suggesting that he come live with him and his new wife, Ethel. His finances had improved after the war, and he promised that he would pay for Jimmy to attend college in California.

Winton Dean's suggestion was an unexpected opportunity, and Jimmy eagerly

Dean became fascinated with auto racing after attending the Indianapolis 500 shortly after his high school graduation.

took advantage of it. However, he would ignore his father's urging that he study law and would instead study acting. He thought he could learn if he had any real talent in nearby Hollywood.

Reverend DeWeerd's graduation present to Jimmy was something that would grip the restless young man for the rest of his life. It was his first trip to the Indianapolis 500 auto races. Jimmy became excited watching the cars as they roared around the track. He began to wonder what it would be like to race one of those cars himself someday.

Leaving the farm and Fairmount and moving to California marked a major turning point in James Dean's life. He embarked on a journey to learn more about himself and what he was capable of achieving through his interest in acting.

Chapter

3 Experiments with Acting and Life

After high school graduation Dean began a new life in California, but despite his father's efforts, Dean continued to feel estranged from him. Hoping to win the approval and love of his father, Dean tried for a movie career. Excited by the new acting style of Marlon Brando on the screen, Dean adopted many of the popular actor's mannerisms. But Dean soon became moody and depressed when he was unable to get any movie roles. Desperate for work and money, he began a relationship with a producer whose influence landed him bit parts in a few movies. But Dean's failed experiments with acting and life left him feeling unhappy. Discouraged, he took the advice of an older actor to go to New York to learn the craft of acting by working in theater.

BACK IN SANTA MONICA

James Dean moved in with his father and stepmother in a small two-bedroom stucco house in Santa Monica in mid-June 1949. He knew right away that the relationship was not going to work. "I knew within five minutes of being back in Santa Monica at my father's house that it was a terrible, rot-

ten mistake,"[44] Dean told his friend John Gilmore a few years later.

Although his father had invited Dean to live with him and his wife and agreed to help him go to college, Dean could not get over the feeling that his father had abandoned him after his mother's death.

Returning to Santa Monica brought conflicting feelings to Dean. He remembered

After high school, Dean went to live with his father and stepmother in Santa Monica, California.

the happy times he had had there with his mother, but he also felt a renewal of the great sense of loss he had felt when she died.

As he had in Indiana, Dean withdrew into himself. He made solitary visits to the neighborhood where he had lived as a child and been happy with his mother. He revisited the library where his mother used to take him and to the park where they had played together in the sand.

TENSIONS AT HOME

In addition to the renewed pain he felt over his mother's death, a rift soon developed between Dean and his father over what subject Dean would major in at college. Winton wanted Dean to become a lawyer, saying that such a career would take full advantage of his talents at debate and recitation, which he had developed in high school.

Winton planned for Dean to enroll as a pre-law student at Santa Monica City College. But Dean's heart and mind were set on becoming an actor, so he insisted on taking drama classes at the University of California at Los Angeles (UCLA).

Just as Winton had disapproved of Dean's playacting as a child, he tried to discourage him from pursuing an acting career by telling him that it was not a manly profession. This further frustrated Dean, but he did not change his mind about becoming an actor.

Disputes over Dean's educational and career future led to tensions at home. It did not help that Dean did not like his stepmother, who he felt criticized him. John Gilmore later recalled,

JIMMY'S FEARS

The death of his mother always troubled and puzzled Jimmy, and he sometimes talked about it to friends. John Gilmore recalled in Live Fast—Die Young, *his biography of Dean, that on one of these occasions Dean said that he did not believe in an afterlife, either a heaven or a hell.*

"If that's the case as you see it, what's the sense?" Gilmore asked.

Dean replied, "It's fear that keeps you going. Fear of being nothing, and fear of having pain. There's nobody I know that isn't afraid of pain."

Gilmore writes, "[Dean] said he hadn't figured it out yet, but he knew there was an answer in it somewhere. It was the kind of answer that kept eluding his search, but it was something he was stuck on, and he figured it had something to do with his mother's death."

Jimmy did not hate the woman who'd replaced his mother, but he couldn't stay in the same room with her without wondering why his mother was dead. [Also], he didn't want to hear his stepmother's "reports" on his father's displeasure with Jimmy's "lack of appreciation." [45]

As it turned out, Dean reluctantly agreed to his father's wish that he study law. He gave in because Winton promised to buy him a used 1939 Chevy sedan if he enrolled in pre-law that fall at Santa Monica City College. Dean agreed and got the car.

Dean's newfound mobility enabled him to spend as much time as he could away from the house that summer to avoid the tensions that continued to arise between himself, his father, and his stepmother. "We were like cats ready to jump on another's back at any moment," [46] he later recalled. Dean found some relief by joining a local summer stock company, where he acted in a musical production of *The Romance of Scarlet Gulch*.

DEAN PLANS FOR HIS FUTURE

That fall Dean tried to apply himself to his pre-law studies at Santa Monica City College, but he softened the burden by taking as many drama classes as he could.

Jean Owen, a drama teacher at Santa Monica, later wrote about Dean's efforts in her class:

He was always polite and thoughtful; his enthusiasm for everything that pertained to the theater was boundless. One day in class, Jimmy read some scenes from Edgar Allan Poe's *Telltale Heart*. He was magnificent— but then he always had a spectacular emotion for any scene he played.

Later, during that same class, I asked Jimmy to read some scenes from *Hamlet*. That night when I returned home I informed my husband that I had finally found the right student to play Hamlet as I felt it should be played. [47]

While Dean played Hamlet convincingly, he was less confident offstage. A fellow drama student later noted, "He was shy and awkward, peering through big horn-rimmed glasses at a world that baffled him." [48]

The tensions between Dean and his father and stepmother continued. Early in the new year, Dean left home and shared an apartment with another student from Santa Monica City College. At the same time, he began to think again of attending the drama school at UCLA. He thought he could appease his father by studying pre-law as his major but minoring in theater arts.

AN ACTING HERO

Young Dean completed his first year of college, and near the end of his summer vacation, he headed back to Indiana to visit his aunt and uncle. While in Indiana, Dean rode his old motorbike into Marion to see a movie he had heard about back in

Los Angeles. A new type of actor, Marlon Brando, was making his screen debut as a paraplegic war veteran in a drama called *The Men*.

Dean immediately identified with Brando's portrayal of a rebel non-conformist. Brando portrayed his character as outwardly serene but inwardly anguished and confused, displaying a complexity that fascinated Dean. He was also impressed by Brando's apparent ability to become the character he was playing. With his skill as a mimic, Dean quickly picked up Brando's slurred way of speaking his lines and casual, slouching manner.

Seeing Brando's intense performance reinforced Dean's determination to become an actor. The best way he saw to make that happen was to enroll in the drama program at UCLA that fall.

DEAN AT UCLA

Winton Dean still disapproved of his son's plan to transfer to UCLA to study acting, but he was unable to change his mind. James Dean transferred to UCLA that fall and majored in theater arts.

Dean got off to a good start at UCLA, and he was ecstatic about landing the supporting role of Malcolm in a UCLA production of Shakespeare's tragedy *Macbeth*. He wrote in his journal, "It's a dream. Don't let anyone wake me up."[49] Instead, Dean had a rude awakening. Despite trying hard

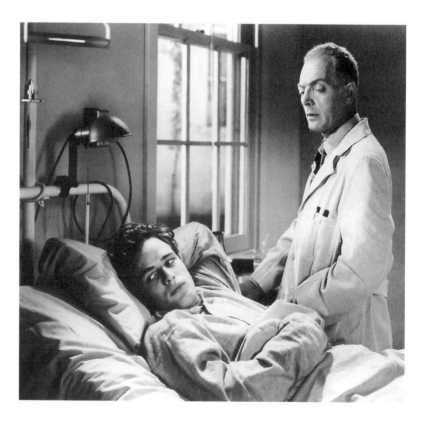

Marlon Brando's portrayal of a paraplegic in The Men *strengthened Dean's desire to become an actor.*

Many people who knew Dean during his college days recalled him as arrogant, moody, and self-absorbed.

in *Macbeth*, the school newspaper panned his performance as lacking maturity.

At about the same time, Dean persuaded a fellow theater arts student, William "Bill" Bast, to pool their meager resources and share an apartment. Even though the rent was more than they could afford, they rented a three-room penthouse in Santa Monica that was near the ocean.

Bast, who had ambitions of becoming an actor but who later became a photographer, recalled living with Dean: "He was cocky and arrogant. He was not an extraordinary person in real life; if any-thing, he was rather bothersome."[50]

Others who knew Dean at the time felt that he was using Bast. John Gilmore said about Dean's relationship with Bast, "The friendship with Bast was momentary—a kind of latching-on—as if each person he encountered could be a rung on some lad-der of opportunity."[51]

Dean's mood swings, from manic to de-pressive, did not make him an easy room-mate. Bast also later recalled of Dean, "He was a very, very stupid boy of his age, but there was also something quite strange about him."[52]

A Young Man Interested in Himself

Many people in Dean's life said that he was self-absorbed. In Live Fast—Die Young, *John Gilmore writes that James Dean himself verified this.*

While still a struggling young actor, Dean met a photographer, Roy Schatt, and "bugged him mercilessly" to teach him photography because he thought it could add to an arsenal of knowledge that would help him in his acting.

"He was a miserable runt who was a genius at posturing a different guise for almost everyone he came in contact with," Gilmore quoted Schatt as saying. "Alone and left alone, he was just that—miserable, a squinty-eyed runt. But he was like an electric bulb—you plug him in and there's all this light. . . . A battery or something inside the person generating this incredible light."

"He wanted me to teach him everything about photography. I said, 'What for? All you're interested in is yourself!'"

Jimmy smiled at him and said, "Who else is going to be looking out for me?"

For his part, Dean saw no reason to modify his behavior to accomodate others. An entry Dean made in his journal at this time reads, "My purpose in life does not include a hankering to charm society."[53]

Dean soon found work because of his roommate. Bast had an after-school and weekend job at the CBS radio production studio in Los Angeles, and he helped Dean become a part-time usher there. However, Dean was soon fired for refusing to conform to the studio's dress code and for refusing to follow orders. However, he got a new job parking cars on the CBS parking lot. Then, in December, he got his first real break.

Dean's Professional Debut

A classmate of Dean's, James Bellah, referred him to Isabelle Draesemer, a Hollywood talent agent. Meeting Dean, Draesemer thought he was just the kind of young man she was looking for to appear in a Pepsi-Cola television commercial she was helping cast. "He had the advantage of being older but looking younger," she recalled. Draesemer also liked his ambiguous manner: "He had a softness one minute and a rebelliousness the next."[54]

Draesemer signed with Dean as his agent and got him a role in the commercial, which paid him thirty dollars. He became one of a group of teenagers dancing around a jukebox singing Pepsi's jingle.

Acting Classes

Encouraged even by this inauspicious start, Dean dropped out of UCLA early in 1951 to pursue a full-time career as an actor. Looking for movie work but finding none, Dean joined an acting workshop given by stage and movie actor James Whitmore. Whitmore saw potential in Dean and encouraged him to attend some of his classes. But he soon discovered what others had, that Dean did not take criticism well. After a few sessions, Dean just did not show up.

Whitmore later recalled that he was aware of an "obvious neurotic strain in [Dean's] personality."[55] Nonetheless, he saw potential in the young man and encouraged Dean to go to New York City and audition for the Actors Studio, the prestigious school for budding actors that had been cofounded in 1947 by the famous director Elia Kazan. Students at the Actors Studio studied a style of acting called "the Method," which emphasized adopting the personality of the character being played. Many top stage and film stars, including Marlon Brando, Montgomery Clift, Julie Harris, Paul Newman, Geraldine Page, Joanne Woodward, and Rod Steiger had attended the Actors Studio and adopted "the Method."

Dean gave some thought to Whitmore's suggestions, but he decided to stay in Los Angeles to pursue television or movie roles. Success was elusive. For one reason or another, Dean lost many parts to other young actors. When he lost one movie role to a taller actor, the casting director told Dean, "You're too pretty. We need a regular guy, and you're too fragile-looking."[56]

The Ups and Downs of a Young Actor

Dean soon got several breaks, however. In March, Jerry Fairbanks, who had been the producer of the Pepsi commercial in which Dean had appeared, offered him a small part in a biblical television drama.

Actor James Whitmore (pictured) encouraged Dean to audition for the Actors Studio in New York City.

Dean earned a much-needed $150 playing the role of the apostle John in "Hill Number One," which aired on Easter Sunday.

Then, in July, Dean's agent got him his first movie role. It was a bit part as a soldier in *Fixed Bayonets*, a Korean War drama about a platoon cut off from the rest of its outfit. Dean was not able to capitalize on this break, however. His one line was later cut from the film before it was released.

When no new work followed, Dean responded by spending his nights drinking in Los Angeles bars. Bill Bast thought his roommate was deeply depressed:

> Jimmy became subject to more frequent periods of depression and would slip off into a silent mood at least once each day. If I had thought it difficult to communicate with him at other times in the past, I had never known such lack of communication as existed during his fits of depression. He sat in the room and stared off into space for hours. I made several attempts to get through to him, but rarely got more than a grunt or a distant stare for a response.[57]

Dean's moodiness disturbed Bast to the point that he decided that he did not want to room with him anymore. Bast moved, leaving Dean, who was broke, to pay the rent by himself.

Bast later said he also stopped living with him because Dean was having an affair with his girlfriend, Beverly Wills. Wills said later of Dean,

> He was almost constantly in a blue funk. He couldn't get an acting job and he was growing increasingly bit-

ter. When he was happy, there was no one more lovable, but when he was depressed, he wanted to die. These low moods became so violent that he began to tell me that he was having strange nightmares in which he dreamed he was dying.

I soon learned that it was nothing for Jimmy to run through a whole alphabet of emotions in one evening. His moods of happiness were by now far outweighed by his moods of deep despair. He was a hurt and misunderstood boy, he thought.[58]

Wills was conflicted about her relationship with Dean, telling a friend, actress

Girlfriend Beverly Wills (pictured) recalled that Dean's bouts with depression outnumbered his periods of happiness.

Marlon Brando and Vivien Leigh in a scene from A Streetcar Named Desire. *Dean tried to imitate Brando in his attitude and acting style.*

Karen Sharpe, "I must be going out of my mind to be seeing this person. I need a psychiatrist or something. He's the worst-mannered and rudest person I've ever dated."[59] Sharpe later observed,

> He'd gotten it into his head that he wanted to be like Marlon Brando, a difficult, rebellious person. I told him Brando had a lot of fame from New York—he'd been a success on Broadway in *A Streetcar Named Desire*. I said, "Brando can afford to act like a jerk, but you're trying to survive—you're trying to get an acting job just to buy a hamburger tomorrow."[60]

How to Succeed in Acting

Dean's low fortunes at this time reached the desperate stage. John Gilmore later said that Dean had told him he needed money to live. Dean also needed to meet people of influence in the movies. In pursuit of both, he hung around bars, nightclubs, hotels, and restaurants frequented by movie people, hoping someone would take an interest in him and give him some acting work.

Gilmore recalled that Dean would attract sympathy by pretending he was a small-town boy lost in the big city: "Almost dull at times or doped up on pot [marijuana], appearing maybe infantile and stubborn, he'd milk the farmboy act to worm his way to advantages."[61]

Jimmy's life at this time also was later recalled by Phil Carey, another struggling young actor. He befriended Dean and remembered that Dean formed relationships with people largely for what he hoped they could do for his career. Carey remembered Dean once telling him, "Getting work is a matter of social politics."[62] But Carey doubted that social politics was really working for Dean: "He was letting himself be used, but he was receiving little of any consequence in return. Jimmy said he had one foot on a treadmill and the other going nowhere."[63]

By this time, Dean was so broke that he was unable to pay rent for an apartment or hotel room. He would sleep in parked cars in the CBS lot.

However, Dean's economic misfortunes were always temporary, as Gilmore later noted: "The discomforts of being broke were short-lived. It didn't have to be a parked car; soon enough it was someone's apartment in Hollywood or a beach house in Malibu."[64]

At least in part, Dean used relationships to further his career. He remembered that his mentor back in Fairmount, Reverend DeWeerd, had encouraged him to experiment with life, and he used that recollection to ease any discomfort he might have felt over the fact that some of these relationships were homosexual. As Dean wrote in his journal, "An actor must learn all there is to know, experience all there is to experience, or approach that state as closely as possible."[65] Bast confirmed this years later, saying he believed Dean was bisexual, adding, "He dabbled in everything. He wanted to experiment with life."[66]

One of Dean's liaisons yielded the opportunity he was looking for. At a party in

A scene from the movie Has Anybody Seen My Gal. *Dean only played a minor role in the film, and felt his acting career was going nowhere.*

the Hollywood hills attended by Liberace, Rock Hudson, and several other celebrities, Dean met Rogers Brackett, a sophisticated and worldly thirty-five-year-old advertising executive who also produced radio shows. Years afterward Brackett said of the relationship they formed, "My primary interest in Jimmy was as an actor. His talent was so obvious. Secondarily, I loved him, and he loved me."[67]

More Bit Parts in Movies

Brackett used his influence with friends in the movie industry, and within weeks he got Dean small roles in three new pictures. The first was a bit part in *Sailor Beware*, a comedy starring Dean Martin and Jerry Lewis. Dean could barely be picked out in a crowd scene that was part of the movie. Dean next worked as an extra in *Trouble Along the Way*, with John Wayne playing a football coach.

Of the three films, Dean's biggest role and most dialog came in the nostalgic comedy set in the 1920s, *Has Anybody Seen My Gal*. In the film, veteran character-actor Charles Coburn starred as a millionaire masquerading as a soda fountain clerk. Dean, playing the part of an annoying teen patron, spoke a few lines trying to get Coburn to make the perfect chocolate malt.

It was hardly a role to bring Dean any critical raves. Discouraged with his lack of success in the movies, Dean felt sorry for himself, writing, "I'm not the bobby-sox type [a happy and untroubled teenager], and I'm not a romantic leading man. They'll never give me a real chance."[68] Dean felt he was on a treadmill, going nowhere with his acting career. Soon, he made a decision to do something about it.

Chapter

4 A New Kind of Teenage Actor

In 1951 Dean moved to New York, but again he found acting roles scarce until he renewed his relationship with a Hollywood producer, who soon got him a part in a Broadway play. Favorable reviews in the play enabled Dean to get parts in television dramas. He experimented further with acting techniques similar to Marlon Brando's, but he put a teenage spin on them, adding his own remembered anxieties as a teenaged loner. Within months he was appearing in dozens of television dramas and began to get noticed as an exciting new young talent. His acting style was so believable that it looked like he was not acting but really was an anguished, misunderstood teenager. By then in his early twenties, Dean was actually playing himself in the television dramas since emotionally he was still a teenager.

A NEW LIFE IN NEW YORK

Discouraged with his movie career in Hollywood, Dean thought of a different approach to becoming a great actor. He had heard it from James Whitmore and several other people in Hollywood: If you want to make it in the movies, first make it on the stage or television in New York. Then Hollywood will come looking for you.

Dean wanted to go to New York but did not have any money to make the trip. The solution to this problem soon came when an advertising agency Rogers Brackett worked for transferred him to Chicago. Dean figured that Chicago was a lot closer to New York than Los Angeles was, so he accepted when Brackett offered to take him along. By September 1951, after a brief stay with Brackett in Chicago, Dean had enough money to travel to New York.

New York City was like a new planet to James Dean. He found himself in one of the largest and fastest-paced cities in the world, and the adjustment, even after living in Los Angeles, was hard.

"New York overwhelmed me," Dean said later. "For the first few weeks I was so confused that I strayed only a couple of blocks from my hotel [the Iroquois] off Times Square. I saw three movies a day in an attempt to escape from my loneliness and depression—spent $150 of my limited funds on movies alone."[69]

Dean also began hanging out at Cromwell's Pharmacy in the lobby of the NBC Building at 30 Rockefeller Plaza. Out-of-work actors frequently went there for coffee, to exchange news about casting calls, and to make phone calls to their agents. To earn some money while waiting for an acting job, Dean worked as a dishwasher in a bar near his hotel.

As he grew accustomed to the city, Dean found that he liked New York very much, as he wrote in his journal, "I've discovered a whole new world here, a whole new way of thinking. . . . This town is the end. It's talent that counts here. You've got to stay with it or get lost. I like it. New York's a fertile, generous city if you can accept the violence and decadence."[70]

Dean also made a new friend in New York City: dancer-actress Elizabeth "Dizzy" Sheridan. They shared an apartment, and after a while Dean suggested that they get married, but she never accepted the proposal. Soon Bill Bast arrived from Los Angeles and joined them in the apartment.

MORE DISAPPOINTMENTS

Months of poverty followed as Dean made the rounds of casting agencies without any success getting work. He enjoyed

Disappointed with his career in Hollywood, Dean moved to New York in hopes of breaking into stage acting or television.

James Dean in New York

"No truer maverick have I ever known. He was a close friend before and during his brief, concentrated movie life. Shortly before his Hollywood recognition, we shared some lean and hungry days in New York, pounding the same pavement in search of the same game [acting work]. On the surface, it seemed the chase was just as important to me as it was to Jimmy, but with hindsight, it is clear he was more determined.

Obsessed with succeeding as an actor—of being crowned the winner—there was little Jimmy would not do to wedge himself into a television role or to get onstage. . . . Almost dull at times or doped up on pot, appearing maybe infantile and stubborn, he'd milk the farmboy act to worm his way to advantages. . . . He got a bang out of dumb pranks [and] jokes about outhouses or jock straps, dreaming up bizarre things to shock and keep an edge on the perverseness that ran right down the middle of him like a core.

We hung around with a few of the same friends for the year in New York; we had sex with the same girls. . . . We even explored sexual experiences with one another. . . . He said you had to be willing to take the chances—the risks. Keep moving ahead, fast, or you wouldn't make the discoveries."

the company of his roommates, but he also suffered bouts of depression.

In moments when his depression lifted, Dean could joke in his journal about the search for work as an actor: "These chairs [in agents' offices] are made scientifically so that in exactly 11 minutes your backside begins to hurt. But I beat the average. First I sit on one half of my fanny, then on the other. They don't get rid of me until my 22 minutes are up. But I'm beginning to take the shape of those chairs. Maybe that's the shape of my destiny."[71]

A Problem for an Actor

Dean had once been told that his delicate good looks were working against him, but he also had another problem that not many other actors competing for roles had: It was difficult for him to read scripts.

According to Dean's friend John Gilmore, Dean once confessed that he was a slow reader. "It takes me a while to get the gist of the whole thing," Dean told him. "Like I have to study what I'm reading."[72] Gilmore elaborated on Dean's reading difficulties:

> It took him a long time to read even one page. He thought in pictures, not words. He would hear poetry read to him and what he'd picture would stay in his mind. He'd remember the pictures and could recite what he'd heard attached to those images.
>
> Reading itself, though, was an excruciating chore and though he'd profess to be an avid reader, a "cosmolite,"

[cosmopolite] as he once put it, he rarely cracked a book. In acting, he had to "swallow the script," as he put it, "take it into the stomach and [let] it out."[73]

THE ACTORS STUDIO

In November, remembering the advice of James Whitmore, Dean auditioned for the Actors Studio. He and a young actress, Christine White, auditioned together in a sketch written by White but with some dialog added by Dean. After performing it, they were among the seven applicants accepted.

It was not long before Dean and the studio's director, Lee Strasberg, clashed over acting philosophies and Dean's inability to

Dean's inability to take criticism put him at odds with Actors Studio director Lee Strasberg (pictured).

take criticism. Dean was told that in Method acting, actors are taught to utilize every emotion from their own lives in playing a part, but never to confuse their lives and those of the characters they play. Dean saw acting as even more personal, requiring that he become the person he played.

Strasberg was known for minutely dissecting an actor's performance during workshops, sometimes spending an hour criticizing a five-minute scene. Never good at taking criticism, Dean rebelled against Strasberg's rigid directing methods, particularly in one class when Dean acted and read lines of a matador preparing for his last bullfight. Dean had always been fasci-nated by bullfighting and thought he performed the scene well. Strasberg disagreed, and his lengthy analysis of Dean's work frustrated the younger man so much that he walked out of the class, determined not to participate in any more readings or performances.

Dean never returned to the Actors Studio. Later, he explained this decision to Bast:

> I don't know what's inside of me. I don't know what happens when I act. . . . But if I let them dissect me, like a rabbit in a clinical research laboratory or something, I might not be able to produce again. They might sterilize me. That man [Strasberg] had no right

DEAN AT THE ACTORS STUDIO

Dean's inability to take criticism gave him serious problems at the Actors Studio, where he had hoped to learn the skills that could make him a great actor. Unable to recognize this flaw in himself, he blamed his frustrations on Lee Strasberg, director of the Actors Studio. He thought Strasberg had a "personal vindictiveness" toward him, favoring other young actors who did not challenge the director's opinions of a performance in class.

John Gilmore quoted Dean in his biography, *Live Fast—Die Young*, saying "Strasberg's ideas are nothing more than personal opinions. It isn't that they are true, only that they're held as being true. [But they're] mostly hot air."

However, Gilmore also quotes John Stix, then head of the Actors Studio board of directors, saying, "Jimmy's self-indulgence wasn't tolerated by Strasberg, nor did he allow Jimmy to use it as a defense against criticism. So Jimmy disliked everyone at the Studio except a couple of people like Kim Stanley and Geraldine Page who tended to allow more margin for his indulgences than did anyone else there."

to tear me down like that. You keep knocking a guy down and you take the guts away from him. And what's an actor without guts?[74]

Dean felt a growing urgency to achieve success as an actor. A new acquaintance, Martin Landau, also a struggling young actor at the time, later recalled,

> Jimmy often said that he had to make it as an actor while he was young. Although we were the same age, [he said] I looked like a man but he would always look like a boy. He used to say that I would grow into myself but he would grow out of himself, so he had to make it before he was thirty.[75]

SMALL SUCCESS, THEN A BIG DECISION

Shortly after Dean left the Actors Studio, a lucky break came along that he hoped would help him toward his goal. Through an acquaintance named James Sheldon, an advertising executive who also directed a few television shows, Dean met an agent who could find him work in New York. "Jimmy was quick and eager," Sheldon recalled, "and he was very hungry to make a mark for himself. It would be a while before I'd be able to actually help him by casting him in something, but I did send him to see an agent I knew—Jane Deacy."[76]

Deacy saw potential in Dean despite his slouch, moody disposition, and the fact that he mumbled the lines she asked him to read. She saw that he also had "a

Dean's need for money forced him to take whatever acting jobs he could get.

bright personality that he could switch on like a big lightbulb."[77]

Deacy believed in Dean's potential as an actor and became his personal manager. He called her "Mom," as did most of her other clients.

Dean told Deacy that he needed money in the worst way and would settle for any acting work she could get him. She asked if he would be interested in helping out on a television quiz show, and he eagerly accepted.

The work Deacy found for Dean was as an assistant on the television quiz show *Beat the Clock*. His job was to act out for the contestants what it was they were expected to do. He sometimes also had to jump up and down like a monkey, scratching himself and imitating monkey calls in order to relax nervous contestants before appearing on the show. Before long, however, Dean was fired because his antics made people even more nervous.

Deacy also got Dean some small parts in television dramas, including "Prologue to Glory," which aired on the *U.S. Steel Hour* that May.

None of the minor roles got Dean the notice he needed, and he soon found himself in need of rent money. When things looked darkest for him both professionally and financially, he left the apartment he shared with Sheridan and Bast. Rogers Brackett had left Chicago and moved to New York by then, and Dean moved into Brackett's luxury apartment on Sunset Plaza Drive.

Both Bast and Deacy cautioned Dean that he might be harmed by a homosexual relationship with Brackett. Rumors of such a relationship, they warned him, could damage his chances of getting work as an actor. Dean, however, said he could take care of himself. He also indicated that he found what he was doing distasteful, saying, "To get to someplace as the crow flies, you got to pass over a lot of crummy territory."[78]

Dizzy Sheridan recalled that Dean admitted using Brackett:

> He told me he met Rogers in a parking lot, that they lived together. Then he told me he was extremely unhappy about what he'd done—that he had "succumbed" to Rogers because he thought [Rogers] could help him. Then he said he didn't want to see

Rogers anymore, but that he had to, to break it off—and that's when he dragged me along to Brackett's apartment and presented me as his girlfriend. And he just hung on to me the whole time. I remember that it pleased him so much that I was very calm and presentable and stoic in front of Rogers Brackett.[79]

But Dean's relationships with both Sheridan and Brackett remained ambiguous. He lived in Brackett's apartment rent-free and let him pay for his dinners and theater tickets. At the same time, he let Sheridan think he was in love with her.

A RETURN TO INDIANA

There were other sides to Dean's personality that he showed when he chose to. As Thanksgiving approached in 1952, Dean persuaded Sheridan and Bast to hitchhike with him to Fairmount and the farm he had grown up on. In rural Indiana, they saw a side of Dean they had never seen before, as he seemed to be more relaxed and happy. Sheridan later recalled, "I wish everyone could have been with us in Indiana to see the way Jimmy treated the animals, even the dirt around the farm. The love he had for nature showed me how completely simple he was."[80] Dean took his friends to his old high school in Fairmount and introduced them to Adeline Brookshire Nall, his former drama teacher. Then he took them to his mother's grave in Marion.

The trip was cut short by a phone call from Rogers Brackett. He had gotten

Dean an audition for a role in a Broadway play. Dean was clearly conflicted over what his next move should be, but he elected to return to New York. Sheridan said that on the bus ride back to Manhattan, "We were very, very depressed, especially going into New York through the tunnel, because we didn't want to get back into the city."[81]

A Success on Broadway

Opportunity finally knocked for James Dean. His audition was a success and he got his first major role in a Broadway play, *See the Jaguar*. Only twenty-one years old then, and looking even younger, Dean played a boy of sixteen whose demented mother keeps him locked in an icehouse all of his life.

While they were working at rehearsals, a fellow actor made a long-lasting impression on Dean. Arthur Kennedy, a movie actor and the star of *Jaguar* who also had been a student of the Actors Studio, stressed the singular importance of the actor.

Alec Wilder, a film music composer who knew both Dean and Kennedy, later recalled Kennedy's influence, which in his view was not necessarily positive:

> I watched [Kennedy] brainwash Jimmy into believing that no one in any production was of any consequence but the actor. I've always believed that this attitude accounted to a great extent for Jimmy's shocking behavior when he hit the big time in Hollywood.[82]

Meanwhile, Kennedy had his own opinion of Dean: "He's the most uniquely talented and peculiar person I've worked with."[83]

Dean's first major role came in the play See the Jaguar. *Although one reviewer praised Dean's performance, the play itself was panned.*

Dean prepared conscientiously for his role in the play, and rehearsals went well until one of the final run-throughs. He got into a fight with one of the stagehands and ended up pulling a switchblade on him. Kennedy broke up the scuffle and calmed down Dean. Dean never explained what had brought on the fight, but others attributed it to an accumulation of nervous tension in the young actor.

During the rehearsals for *Jaguar*, Dean became friends with one of the other cast members, Barbara Glenn. Glenn later described how Dean appeared to her at the time: "He was physically gorgeous, with a lost quality about him that immediately touched me. It was as though he was the only person in the world, totally unattached to anything or anyone."[84]

Dean and the rest of the cast of See the Jaguar *celebrated the play's opening at Sardi's, a posh Manhattan restaurant.*

Others noticed that Dean exhibited childlike qualities. Phillip Pine, also acting in *Jaguar*, recalled, "[Dean] was completely taken with his own momentary need. Everything was judged by 'What do I feel *now*.' He was undisciplined." Pine then added, "But I never met anyone who was more appealing to the maternal sense in all women."[85]

When *Jaguar* finally opened, Dean was thrilled by what he thought was a positive reaction to the play. Ecstatic, he took Sheridan and Bast with him to the cast party at a posh restaurant in Manhattan. Dean was on an emotional high there, almost dancing around the room from table to table, soaking up praise.

Dean's elation, however, was short-lived. Newspapers the next morning contained unfavorable reviews by most of the critics.

Despite negative reviews of the play itself, Dean took some solace in Walter Kerr's review in the *New York Times* that read, in part,

> James Dean adds an extraordinary performance in an almost impossible role: that of a bewildered lad who has been completely shut off from a vicious world by an over-zealous mother, and who is coming upon both the beauty and brutality of the mountain for the first time.[86]

Despite that good review of his work in *Jaguar*, Dean took criticism of the play personally, as though it had been criticism of him. Considering himself a failure as an actor, Dean again withdrew into himself. Dizzy Sheridan noticed his

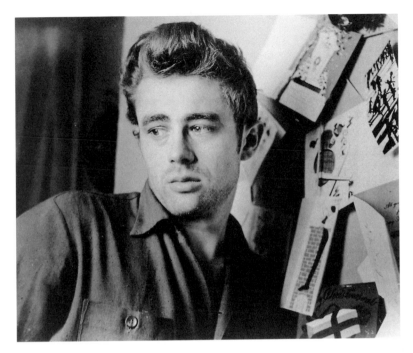

Despite Dean's desire to succeed as an actor, his behavior seemed aimed at alienating the people who could help him the most.

behavior at this time: "He didn't care about the way he dressed. Sometimes he didn't even care about whether he was decent to people or not, as long as he was acting. He seemed in even a worse condition, more hard and bitter than before."[87]

Jimmy spent more time alone that winter. By then he had enough money to leave Rogers Brackett's apartment, and he rented a room at the Iroquois Hotel. But Dean continued to visit Brackett and to attend his parties, still hoping to meet someone who would give him his big break in acting. When Dean was unable to sleep, which was often, he played sad melodies that he composed on a recorder.

When Sheridan would visit him in his hotel room, she would find him in need of comforting. She later recalled that he would cling to her, "all bunched up in my arms, and it was like I was rocking him to sleep—like it was going to be painful for him to get up in the morning and have to face another day having to do what he was doing."[88]

"Being an actor is the loneliest thing in the world," he told his agent, Jane Deacy, that winter. "You're all alone with your imagination, and that's all you have."[89] Oddly, Dean's actions seemed designed to alienate those who might have helped him. When he was greeted by acquaintances in restaurants or at auditions, he ignored them or pretended he did not know them.

Broke again and unable to pay the weekly rent at the Iroquois, Dean packed his things into an army duffel bag he used as a suitcase. Reluctantly, he moved back in with Rogers Brackett.

Disappointed with his role in The Immoralist, *starring Geraldine Page and Louis Jourdan (pictured), Dean quit the play giving only two weeks' notice.*

EN ROUTE TO THE BIG BREAK

Dean's work as an actor was being noticed, though. On the strength of his performance in *Jaguar*, Deacy found work for him in thirty live television dramas during most of 1953. He gained valuable experience working with famous actors, including Dorothy Gish, Jessica Tandy, and Hume Cronyn, as well as one of the top television writers, Rod Serling. Dean's reputation as an actor was growing, but he also began to get a reputation for being difficult. A director of one of the televi-

sion dramas said that Dean was often moody on the set and usually just sat by himself: "At rehearsals he would mumble his words as though completely disinterested in them. But, like Brando, the moment the camera was on him, he came across."[90]

Success brought Dean the money he needed. With some of his television earnings, Dean bought a motorcycle on which he raced around the crowded streets of Manhattan. Barbara Glenn was fearful about Dean's motorcycle riding, later saying,

I considered it [the motorcycle] an instrument of death. I remember half of my life with Jimmy was waiting for him because he was always late, and I was always wondering if he was going to make it. I always had the feeling that somehow, some way, some day he's not going to show up.[91]

Dean crashed the motorcycle a year later, but without hurting himself.

Early in 1954 Dean returned to the Broadway stage. He wore dark makeup to play a thieving, blackmailing homosexual Arab houseboy in *The Immoralist*, an intellectual play based on a novel by the unconventional French writer, André Gide. The play starred Geraldine Page and Louis Jourdan.

Dean's old problem of being unable to read scripts returned, but Page later recalled that in some mysterious way, Dean overcame his disability:

Jimmy's difficulties at dealing with the printed page somehow bypassed some other part of him, triggering the most intense concentration of any actor I've ever worked with. He was like a cat that jumps a great distance without the need to know how far he has to jump.[92]

Jourdan, however, was exasperated with Dean for mumbling his lines incomprehensibly and muttering obscenities at rehearsals. He recalled that working with Dean was the worst experience he had had in the theater and called him a "monster."[93] Daniel Mann, who directed *The Immoralist*, also was critical of Dean's manner of dealing with his colleagues, saying, "Jimmy had no graciousness, or politeness, or concern on stage."[94]

Although Dean antagonized the play's producers and director by being impatient and critical, he gave what many said was a brilliant performance when it opened in Philadelphia. Critics especially noted a seductive dance that Dean performed in the play while wearing a long robe and clicking a pair of castanets.

Reviews of *The Immoralist* were good in Philadelphia, but producer Billy Rose was not satisfied with the play and called for rewrites. Dean became discouraged when he saw his part becoming smaller. After appearing in the play on opening night on Broadway, he gave two weeks' notice to quit the show in order to look for other work that might satisfy him more. Despite his short run in the play, later that year he won the Daniel Blum Award as the year's most promising personality in a Broadway play.

A week after leaving *The Immoralist*, Dean began rehearsals for a role in *Women of Trachis*, by the classical Greek playwright Sophocles. But before the play opened, the break that every young actor works for and dreams of came Dean's way.

During his three years in New York, the dozens of television shows that Dean had appeared in finally got him noticed in Hollywood. Now Dean was being thought of as an exciting if raw new actor in the mold of Marlon Brando, although about ten years younger. This was soon to lead Dean into the most exciting phase of his life.

Chapter

5 Success but No Peace

Dean's television and stage work in New York came to the attention of stage and movie director Elia Kazan, who directed Marlon Brando in his great success *A Streetcar Named Desire*. Kazan saw a younger version of Brando in the enigmatic Dean and cast him in a lead role in his new movie, *East of Eden*. Both on and off of the movie set, Dean came to personify a young, anguished rebel and loner. But success, Dean came to realize, did not solve his personal problems.

THE BIG BREAK

Success beyond even Dean's imagination soon came his way. In March 1954, while Dean was rehearsing the stage play *Women of Trachis* in New York City, Elia Kazan was searching for a young actor to play the lead in his new motion picture, *East of Eden*.

Based on John Steinbeck's best-selling Depression-era novel, the movie was about the intense conflict between two brothers for the love of their father after their mother had deserted the family. The most challenging role in the movie was that of Cal Trask, who was anguished be-

cause he knew his father preferred his brother. Kazan had Dean in mind to play Cal.

Dean's big break had come because Paul Osborn, whom Kazan had chosen to write the screenplay for *East of Eden*, had seen him in *The Immoralist* and had urged Kazan to see it, too. Kazan had observed Dean in classes at the Actors Studio and not been impressed, but seeing him in *The Immoralist* changed his opinion.

Inviting Dean to an interview at Warner Brothers' New York office, Kazan later recalled,

> He looked and spoke like the character [Cal] in *East of Eden*. When he walked into the office, I knew immediately that he was right for the role. He was guarded, sullen, suspicious, and he seemed to me to have a great deal of concealed emotion.[95]

As Dean had done back in Indiana with classmates at school, he played daredevil with Kazan. He maneuvered the director into going on a wild motorcycle ride with him through Manhattan. Rather than alienating him, the risky stunt further convinced Kazan that Dean was right to play Cal. Kazan also saw how troubled Dean was:

> He had his own way, and I thought he was perfect for the part [of Cal]. I thought he was an extreme grotesque of a boy, a twisted boy. As I got to know his father, as I got to know about his family, I learned that he had been, in fact, twisted by the denial of love.[96]

Although Kazan recognized acting qualities in Dean that he had seen in Marlon Brando, there was a big difference between the two actors when it came to depth. John Gilmore later noted,

According to Kazan, Brando had a "whole array of emotions to draw upon," a vast and varied field of sensations and conflicting emotions. Whereas Jimmy, he would later say, had "this one hurt," a kind of storehouse loaded with a single emotion, a deep hurt embedded and struggling within him.

"It was what made people want to mother him," Kazan says, "that made the girls and boys want to put their arms around him and tell him it was okay, that he'd be all right after all,

Dean's performance in The Immoralist *impressed director Elia Kazan (pictured), who cast him as Cal Trask in* East of Eden.

that they would take care of him, guard him, protect him."[97]

For once, Jimmy's good looks helped him land a part. Kazan was aware of them, later saying, "His face is so desolate and lonely and strange. And there are moments when you say, 'Oh, God, he's handsome!'"[98]

Kazan also had been taken by Dean's physical grace. Larry Swindell, who attended Santa Monica City College with Dean, said, "Kazan told me he was first attracted by Dean's wonderful use of a very athletic body and that body-acting is a natural faculty that can't be taught." Dean's first agent, Isabel Draesemer, agreed: "To me, his sex appeal lay in his mouth and below—the use of his body."[99]

Kazan was impressed by Dean's acting ability and looks, but he was aware of Dean's obvious flaws:

> I got to know him, and he was an absolutely rotten person. But he was the most perfect actor for that part [of Cal Trask]—all bound up in himself and his neurotic problems, lashing out at inappropriate moments. There wasn't any question in my mind that he'd bring it off—all he had to do was be himself.[100]

Dean was a sensation in his screen test and Warner Brothers signed him to a nine-picture contract. His salary for *East of Eden* would be ten thousand dollars, with an increase for each picture until it reached forty thousand dollars on the ninth film.

Besides his acting ability, Dean's physical grace impressed director Elia Kazan.

A STILL-DISTANT FATHER

Dean was excited about going to Hollywood with Kazan for several reasons. For one thing, it meant his first ride in an airplane. For another, he planned to see his father in Santa Monica and tell him of his good fortune being cast in a leading role in a major motion picture with an important director.

Dean and Kazan flew together to Hollywood on April 8. The director was surprised and amused that his new actor brought no luggage with him. Dean carried his few possessions aboard in a brown paper package tied with string.

Upon their arrival in Hollywood, en route to the Warner Brothers studio, Dean asked if they could stop so that he could see his father. He hoped it would impress his father that he was now signed to make a big movie directed by the great Elia Kazan.

However, the meeting proved to be brief and Winton Dean showed no sign of being impressed. Kazan later recalled the meeting at Winton's home:

> Out came a man who was as tense as Jimmy was, and they hardly could look at each other. They could hardly talk; they mumbled at each other. I don't know what Jimmy stopped to see him for, because in a few minutes he said, "Let's go."[101]

Dean was to draw on his feelings for his real-life father in playing Cal Trask. "The grudges against his father, so embedded in Jimmy, were overwhelmingly brought into focus in *East of Eden*, and millions would respond to its impact," John Gilmore later said. "Kazan knew this — it was what he was working towards."[102]

A New Rebel in Hollywood

James Dean was indeed something new in Hollywood, and Kazan also knew that. Before filming began on *East of Eden*, Kazan felt a need to prepare the cast for him.

Actor Dennis Hopper, who was Dean's age and who was cast in a minor role in the film, recalls that Kazan told them, "You're going to meet a boy, and he's going to be very strange to you and he's gonna be

---

Acclaim for Dean in *East of Eden*

East of Eden was highly praised and Dean's performance was acclaimed by most critics. In *James Dean: the Biography*, Val Holley reports that Hedda Hopper, one of the leading movie columnists, said Dean's performance had "such power, so many facets of expression, and so much sheer invention [he is] the brightest star in town."

Mike Connolly, another top movie columnist, agreed, calling Dean "Hollywood's brightest new star." He said Dean's performance in *East of Eden* "puts him at the very top with the all-time greats."

East of Eden brought James Dean overnight stardom as well as an Oscar nomination and more public adulation, especially from teenage girls, than he ever wished for.

different; no matter what you see or what you think of him, when you see him on the screen he's gonna be pure gold."[103]

Once on the set, Dean wasted no time putting into practice advice he had once gotten from Arthur Kennedy, which was to take over any production he was in. By doing that, however, Dean alienated Raymond Massey, a distinguished veteran actor who played the unloving father in *Eden*. Massey considered Dean to be unprofessional and disrespectful to those with more experience in movies. For one thing, Massey was impatient with how much time Dean took preparing for a scene, and Dean's lackadaisical and often rude manner irritated him. Also, Dean frequently changed his dialog from what appeared in the script, which confused Massey and the other actors. "Make him say the lines the way they're written!"[104] Massey would anguish to Kazan.

Kazan responded by fanning the flames of Dean's and Massey's dislike of each other. As he later said,

> I let Jimmy say his lines the way he wanted—just because it irritated Massey! Would I do anything to stop that antagonism? No—I increased it, I let it go! It was the central thing in the story. What I photographed [in the

Dean's attitude quickly alienated everyone on the set, particularly Raymond Massey (right), who played Cal Trask's father in East of Eden.

Dean is seen here with costars Richard Davalos and Julie Harris in a scene from East of Eden. *When not filming, Dean avoided his colleagues and kept to himself.*

movie] was the absolute hatred of Raymond Massey for James Dean, and of James Dean for Raymond Massey. That was precious. No director could get it in any other way.[105]

The friction between Massey and Dean in real life transferred to the screen as great drama. Moreover, beneath the tension between Cal and his father was Dean's inner frustration that he had been rejected by his own father.

While Kazan encouraged the feud between Massey and Dean, he also found himself clashing with his temperamental protégé during the filming of *Eden*. Kazan said years later, "Jimmy Dean was a very difficult and most times a thoroughly impossible character. He fought with fellow artists and the crew and tried to ruin [costar] Julie Harris's good scenes."[106]

Dean's personal insecurities and his inability to take criticism led him to alienate almost everyone working on the film. He kept to himself when off the set, and he would not join other young actors and actresses at restaurants or parties so they could be photographed.

Dean, always an outsider and loner, remained so during the filming of *Eden*. Director Nicholas Ray, who later worked with Dean, recalled, "Everything Jimmy did suggested he had no intention of belonging to the place [Hollywood]. He shied away from social convention, from manners, because they suggested disguise."[107]

Dean felt more comfortable in New York, so he wanted to get through *East of Eden* as quickly as he could. As he wrote in his journal, "I want to make this picture and get back to New York."[108]

ACTING IN HOLLYWOOD

Despite his aversion for the phoniness he saw among movie people, Dean could put on an act himself. One night while in a drugstore near the Warner Brothers studio, he ran into a former girlfriend, Karen Sharpe, who was then also working in a picture at the studio. Someone then came into the drugstore whom Dean knew, and Sharpe recalled, "He did act strangely—brooding, incoherent, and staring into his coffee, not looking up. Later I came to understand that his notorious 'strangeness' was just an act. But he played that part so long, maybe he became the act."[109]

A STUDIO ROMANCE

During filming of *Eden*, Dean was introduced to the ways of what is called "Hollywood dating." Young actors are often asked to go on dates arranged by their studios for publicity purposes.

Terry Moore, an actress Dean reluctantly began dating at his studio's insistence for publicity purposes, said she had the same opinion of his behavior: "I believed his mannerisms were premeditated. I think his behavior was an act."[110] Moore invited Dean to her parents' home for dinner one night. Later she said, "My father never recovered from the shock of watching Jimmy unzip his pants and let out a belch after dinner."[111]

Still, Moore did not object when Dean began following her around, and she went on more dates with him. But photos of them together at movie openings showed how little the relationship meant to Dean. While she smiled at the camera,

At his studio's insistence, Dean briefly dated actress Terry Moore as a way of generating publicity.

Dean looked bored. For his part, Dean thought he meant very little to Moore: "She just went with me for the publicity, and I don't know why . . . I let [the studio] talk me into it."[112]

A LOVE AFFAIR

It was during the final days of filming *East of Eden* that Dean fell in love for the first time, or at least believed he had. Pier Angeli, a beautiful young actress also working at Warner Brothers, was starring opposite Paul Newman in his debut film, *The Silver Chalice*. However, Hollywood gossip columnists wondered if the Dean–Angeli romance was just another attempt by the studio to generate publicity for them and the movies they were working on.

Despite the doubts of gossip columnists, the relationship appeared to be serious, but Angeli's mother disapproved of the romance. She considered Dean rude and unkempt; moreover, he was not a Catholic. As it turned out, after a short time Angeli ended the relationship, choosing instead to marry singer Vic Damone. Years later, Pier Angeli spoke of how she felt about Dean:

> He wanted me to love him unconditionally, but Jimmy was not able to love someone else in return, that is with any deep feeling for that other person. He wanted to be loved. It was the troubled boy that wanted to be loved very badly.
>
> I loved Jimmy as I have loved no one else in my life, but I could not give him the enormous amount that he needed. It emptied me. There was no other way to be with Jimmy except to love him and be emptied of yourself. [113]

How Dean actually felt is uncertain. Biographer John Gilmore later wrote, "Jimmy never had it in mind to marry Pier. He faked it. He was more concerned about the horse he'd bought and what it ate." [114]

Publicly, however, Dean pined for his lost love. He went to Pier Angeli's wedding to Vic Damone on November 23, 1954, in a black leather jacket she hated him wearing, sat on his motorcycle outside the church, and reportedly gunned its engine during the ceremony. But Dean also turned to a new love—a fast new white 356 1500cc Porsche Spyder Speedster convertible, and he began entering car races.

THE END OF EDEN

Despite wanting to return to New York, Dean was sorry when the filming of *East*

Dean's brief relationship with actress Pier Angeli ended when she chose to marry singer Vic Damone.

of Eden was completed on August 9, 1954, after ten weeks of shooting. Costar Julie Harris looked for him on the set, hoping to say good-bye. She was surprised to find Dean alone in his dressing room.

"'Surely he can't be alone,'" Harris later said she recalled thinking.

> And I knocked on the door. Nothing happened. So I kept knocking. And he opened the door and he was all red-eyed and crying. And he said, "It's all over. It's all over." I said, "Oh, I didn't know anyone could feel that except myself." He said, "It's all over." He was just like a child.[115]

Worried about what might happen to the star of his movie, Kazan had forbidden Dean from riding his motorcycle during filming of *Eden*. After finishing work on the picture, Dean bought a new and more powerful motorcycle, a Triumph 500, and began racing it around Los Angeles.

A FLAWED SUCCESS

Despite rumors that he was a huge hit in *Eden*, Dean remained withdrawn after filming finished. When the movie premiered in New York in 1954, he stayed away. He had been in New York, but he took a plane back to Los Angeles to escape the event. "Why should I go [to the premiere]?," he had asked a friend. "I know I was good, and having people tell me so would only embarrass me."[116] Critics were almost unanimous in their praise of Dean and of the picture. Audiences, especially young girls wailing in their seats, lost their hearts to him.

Kazan knew how fortunate he had been to cast James Dean as Cal Trask. Twenty years after filming *East of Eden*, Kazan recalled casting Dean:

> I was lucky. I mean, how lucky can you get? He was *it*. He didn't even have to act. . . . He was never more

---

JAMES DEAN ON ACTING

Dean took acting seriously and equated it with living, as he wrote in his journal, entries from which appear in Neil Grant's James Dean: In His Own Words.

"To grasp the full significance of life is the actor's duty; to interpret it his problem; and to express it his dedication.

Being an actor is the loneliest thing in the world. You are all alone with your concentration and imagination, and that's all you have.

Being an actor isn't easy. Being a man is even harder. I want to be both before I'm done."

Elia Kazan, pictured here with Marlon Brando, Julie Harris, and James Dean, often compared Brando and Dean, saying that Brando was troubled but Dean was sick.

than a limited actor, a highly neurotic young man. But he had a lot of talent, and he worked like hell. He was very completely involved, I'll say that. And he was the perfect boy for the part. He did a swell job, you know." [117]

Kazan, who later said he did not in fact like Dean, compared him to Marlon Brando:

And yet Dean was obviously sick. I don't know what was the matter with him. He got more so. . . . But I'd rather not talk about him. . . . He was not like Brando. Dean was a cripple . . . inside. He was a far, far sicker kid, he was so sick and twisted. And Brando's not sick, he's just troubled. [118]

Frightened by Success

Dean's overnight success in *East of Eden* brought pressures he never dreamed of. He was still very young and had trouble coping with being thrust into the role of public icon. As he wrote in his journal, "It's . . . just . . . that . . . I . . . am frightened. Frightened by this success. It's all come too early for me." [119]

As *Eden* became a box-office hit and Dean's fan mail poured into the Warner Brothers mail room at a rate of a thousand letters a week, studio officials were eager to put him in a new movie. Neither they nor Dean could guess that his next role would cause an even greater sensation and a new cult would be born—the cult of James Dean.

Chapter

6 Personification of a Teenage Rebel

Right after finishing work on *East of Eden*, Dean starred as a 1950s teenager in *Rebel Without a Cause*. Previews of the movie resulted in him becoming an overnight movie sensation, especially with teenagers who identified with the troubled youth he portrayed. However, Dean continued to be plagued by long-standing personal anxieties, and career success did not bring him the solace and the self-esteem he sought.

MORE TEEN REALISM

Director Nicholas Ray, who had made *They Live by Night*, a film about teenagers in trouble with the law, became interested in creating a film version of a novel he had heard about, one that portrayed teenagers more realistically than previous books or movies had. *Rebel Without a Cause*, by Robert M. Lidner, was the story of Jim Stark, a defiant teenager fighting hypocrisy he saw in members of his family and in society.

Ray saw in James Dean the actor he needed for his film. "I had seen *East of Eden*, had met Jimmy, and knew he was the ideal actor for Stark,"[120] Ray later recalled. He was even more convinced after meeting Dean in New York and learning about his personal life:

> The drama of his life, I thought, after seeing him in New York, was the drama of desiring to belong and of fearing to belong. So was Jim Stark's. It

After watching East of Eden, *director Nicholas Ray chose Dean to play the lead role of Jim Stark in* Rebel Without a Cause.

In Rebel Without a Cause, *Sal Mineo and Natalie Wood were cast as teenagers who became a substitute family for the troubled and rebellious Jim Stark.*

was a conflict of violent eagerness and mistrust created very young. The intensity of his desires, his fears, could make the search at times arrogant, egocentric; but behind it was such a desperate vulnerability that one was moved, even frightened.[121]

Although Dean wanted a rest after completing *East of Eden*, he liked the concept of *Rebel* and agreed to do the film. As Jim Stark, he would play the part of a boy who had gotten into trouble despite his solid upbringing. Even though Dean was by that time twenty-four, he looked young enough to be seventeen. His role would be that of a son of a weak middle-class father and a domineering mother. Neither parent understood their son, so he formed a sub-

stitute family with high school friends Judy and Plato. Natalie Wood, then sixteen, was cast as Judy and Plato was played by Sal Mineo, then fifteen.

The mother in *Rebel* was played by veteran character actress Ann Doran. Before filming, Dean tested her as he had others by taking her on a wild motorcycle ride. In spite of the terror she felt, Doran and Dean became friends.

Prior to filming, Ray only had a superficial concept of the character of Jim Stark and he hoped Dean could bring him to life. To help him develop his role, Ray urged Dean to probe his own emotional experiences and go out on the streets to meet troubled teenagers. Dean later recalled that what he learned was both suprising and disturbing:

DEAN ON THE IMPORTANCE OF *REBEL WITHOUT A CAUSE*

In an interview at a preview of Rebel Without a Cause, *Dean discussed what he thought was the picture's meaning and importance.*

"I think the one thing this picture shows that's new is the psychological disproportion of the kids' demands on the parents. Parents are often at fault, but the kids have some work to do, too.

But you can't show some far off idyllic conception of behavior if you want the kids to come and see the picture. You've got to show what it's really like, and try to reach them on their own grounds.

I hope [the picture] will remind them that other people have feelings. If a picture is psychologically motivated, if there is truth in the relationship in it, then I think that picture will do good. I firmly believe *Rebel Without a Cause* is such a picture."

I went out and hung around with kids in Los Angeles before making the movie. . . . They wear leather jackets, go out looking for someone to rough up a little. These aren't poor kids, you know. Lots of them have money, grow up and become pillars of the community. Boy, they scared me![122]

DEAN BECOMES JIM STARK

Filming began in black and white, with Dean wearing a brown jacket and glasses. Then Warner Brothers executives became excited by the rave reviews and teen girls' adoring reaction to Dean when *East of Eden* was released just a week later. Deciding that *Rebel* would be a more important film than they had expected, they

told Ray to take the glasses off Dean and start over, this time shooting in color. Costume designer Moss Mabry said Dean should wear a screaming red nylon windbreaker that would make him stand out.

Ray encouraged Dean to improvise during filming and to offer ideas for developing the character of Jim Stark. It soon became obvious to everyone on the set that James Dean *was* the teenage rebel. Stewart Stern, who wrote the screenplay for the movie, said it became obvious that Dean did not want to play Jim Stark in the film; he wanted to play himself: "He was trying to get out of the role he felt he was being shoved into, whether as a son or a bad boy. Whatever it was, he wanted to be *himself*."[123]

When the time came to perform in front of the camera, Dean prepared in his own unorthodox way. Ann Doran recalled what he did before one scene:

> Jimmy dropped to the floor in the fetal position for the longest time, chin and knees together, holding his legs—still on his feet, but as close to the floor as he could get without lying on it. Finally, came this weak little whistle [from him] and he stood up, ready to do the scene, which he'd rehearsed once, in a single take.[124]

All of the cast members felt Dean's intensity in playing Jim Stark. Dean had grown as an actor since making *Eden*, and he took on the role of elder statesman to his peers on the film. He advised Dennis Hopper, who was playing the part of a fellow gang member, "Don't *act*. If you're smoking a cigarette, smoke it. Don't act like you're smoking it." He went on, "When you know there is something more to go in a character, and

During the filming of Rebel, *Dean became friends with his coworkers, including veteran actress Ann Doran (pictured), who played the role of Jim Stark's mother.*

you're not sure what it is, you just got to go out after it. Walk on a tightrope."[125]

Dean, although critical of some aspects of his performance, was generally happy with his experience, as he noted in his journal after seeing a sneak preview of the film:

> I put everything I had into that one, and I'm pleased with the general result. Any writer, musician, painter or actor will tell you that when they look back on their work they know it could be improved. But in the end you have to say OK, that's it, it's finished—it stands or falls as it is.

> I now regard Natalie [Wood], Nick [Ray], and Sal [Mineo] as co-workers. I regard them as friends . . . about the only friends I have in this town.[126]

On this set, Dean did not alienate his coworkers the way he had in *East of Eden*. In fact, Natalie Wood recalled of him,

> He was so inspiring, always so patient and kind. He didn't act as though he were a star at all. We all gave each other suggestions and he was very critical of himself, never satisfied with his work, and worried about how every scene would turn out. He was so great when he played a scene, he had the ability to make everyone else look great too.

> He used to come on the set and watch the scenes even when he wasn't in them. He was that interested in the whole picture and not just his own part.[127]

Sal Mineo was lavish in crediting Dean for making the film work: "Something happened during the making of that picture for everybody. It wasn't just making a movie. It was as close to a spiritual ex-

Dean's intensity during the filming of Rebel *won him the praise and admiration of his costars.*

Racing his sports car helped Dean feel some relief from the pressure that came along with fame.

perience as you can get. And Jimmy was the focus, the center of it all. It all happened because of him."[128]

Dean professed not to care what the critics said of the film or his work on it. He did not like or trust reporters or movie columnists and granted few interviews. "I don't care what people write about me," he said. "I'll talk to [reporters] I like. The others can print whatever they please. . . . What counts to the artist is performance, not publicity. Guys who don't know me, already they've typed me as an oddball."[129]

A CRY FOR HELP

The pressures of his work and the new fame it was bringing him kept Dean awake at night. During the filming of

Rebel, Dean had begun seeing a psychiatrist three times a week, mainly for treatment of his insomnia.

Dean, however, was not a cooperative patient. Just as he had resented criticism from directors, Dean resisted exposing his feelings to his psychiatrist. Dean wrote in his journal, "Whatever's inside making me what I am, it's like film. Film only works in the dark. Tear it all open and let in the light and you'll kill it."[130] Moreover, he felt that the psychiatrist was telling him nothing new. As he told his fellow cast member Nick Adams, "They say for me to love my father. I could have told them that fifteen years ago."[131]

Dean sought relief from his anxieties in racing his sports car at tracks in Southern California. "Racing is the only time I feel whole,"[132] he wrote in his journal. He drove in five races before his studio put a stop to his racing until he finished making *Rebel*. Others in Hollywood thought that Dean thrived on a certain amount of risk. Actor Rip Torn later said, "Racing allowed him to live life on the edge."[133]

ANOTHER LOSS

When the filming of *Rebel Without a Cause* ended on May 26, 1955, Dean experienced another sense of great personal loss, as he had after completing *Eden*. Nicholas Ray remembered,

> Jimmy and I were alone on the lot at Warners; everyone but the gate man had gone home. We were wandering around under the lights making sure we hadn't left anything behind. We didn't really want to admit it was all over. I said, "Let's go. We've nothing more to do here."

> Dean climbed onto his motorbike and I climbed in my car and we raced into town very fast. On Hollywood Boulevard he spread himself like a flying angel on the bike with his feet up on the back mudguard, his arms outstretched, and sped off with a roar.[134]

Dean resisted the breakup of the cast once filming ended. About a week after the movie was completed, Ann Doran was awakened at home around three o'clock in the morning by cries of "Mom! Mom!" Looking out a window into the darkness, she could not tell who the man was standing on her front lawn yelling up to her. "Who's there?" she asked out the window. "It's your son, Jimmy!"[135] a drunken Dean called back. She let him in and, giving him black coffee, listened to him pour out his heart about his loneliness and fears.

It was obvious to those who knew him: Dean was happiest when he was acting. It was what made him feel free. As he wrote in his journal, "I think all of us have a great need to let go. Acting is my outlet."[136]

One of Dean's fears, not suprisingly, was of death. A biographer, Joe Hyams, says that one night while Dean drove him at high speed around Los Angeles, the young actor talked about a dream he had about his mother:

> In the dream I was a child, and my mother was calling to me. We were in a desert and I tried to run to her but my feet kept plunging into the sand. With each step I took toward her she seemed to drift away so the distance between us was constant no matter how hard I ran. She was trying to say something to me—something I knew was important—but I was never able to get close enough to hear her words clearly. Then I awoke from the dream with the sensation of falling. Does it mean I am going to die soon?[137]

Hyams replied, "Only if you insist on driving flat out on curves like these."[138]

THE INSECURITIES OF AN ACTOR

Dean's anxieties only grew more pronounced as his next picture loomed. His first two movies had been small compared to his next assignment. While he was still working on *Rebel*, Warner Brothers signed him to costar with two of Hollywood's top stars at the time, Elizabeth Taylor and Rock Hudson, in an epic film called *Giant*. It was to be the studio's big picture of the year, a planned three-hour-and-twenty-minute movie spanning almost thirty years in the life of a Texas family. Filming was to begin immediately after completion of *Rebel*.

Dean was to play a cowhand jealous of cattle baron Hudson's wealth and his beautiful wife, played by Taylor. The film presented Dean with a challenge: His part called for him to age and mature from a rebellious poor young man in his twenties to an oil tycoon in his fifties. Dean had never played any but teenaged characters. He wondered how he would do that.

Dean had heard about the project while filming *Rebel*, and despite his anxieties, he was eager to play in it. He believed an Elizabeth Taylor movie directed by one of Hollywood's most respected directors, George Stevens, could be good for his career. He got the role of rebellious misfit Jett Rink in *Giant* by frequently visiting Stevens's office on the Warner lot and telling him how right he would be for the part.

REBEL WITHOUT A CAUSE IS STILL IMPORTANT

Over forty years after Rebel Without a Cause *was released, Jeanine Basinger, a professor of film studies at Wesleyan University in Middletown, Connecticut, describes its importance to teenagers then and now in the article* "Remembering Rebel" *for the October 1999 issue of* American Movie Classics Magazine.

"*Rebel* spoke directly to teens in 1955 because it presented a point of view they recognized as their own. The film rang true emotionally, setting up the world of teenagers as a separate universe. It treated their pain seriously, respecting it, instead of turning it into the subject for cute little comedies about 'growing up.'

Rebel hit home because the teens in it understood their situation at a level the adults couldn't even imagine. America, the old prewar version, was going to pieces slowly and quietly, but only the young could see it was happening. . . .

Every teenager in the audience got the message. *Rebel* definitely spoke to its own times, but even today . . . audiences can still feel what made it a top box-office draw and earned it three Oscar nominations: about teenagers, it was sincere. As Natalie Wood tells Sal Mineo, 'Well, that's the main thing, isn't it? Being sincere.'"

A Nervous Star

Dean was nervous and unsure of himself when *Giant* began filming. On Dean's first day in front of the cameras, Stevens was directing him and Taylor on location at a Texas ranch with most of the twenty-five hundred residents of the nearby town of Marfa watching in the hot sun near the Mexican border. Stevens was not satisfied and reshot the scene several times.

Dean was feeling the pressures of acting in the first big picture of his career, with a legendary director and one of Hollywood's top actresses. Before Stevens could shoot the scene again, Dean walked off the set, faced the crowd, opened his jeans, and urinated. He then calmly returned to the set and told Stevens, "Okay, let's go. I'm ready."[139]

Dennis Hopper, who played Rock Hudson's son in *Giant*, later quoted Dean justifying the action that shocked everyone present:

> "I was nervous. If you're nervous your senses can't reach your subconscious, and that's that—you just can't work. So I figured if I could [urinate] in front of all those people, and be cool about it, I could go in front of the camera and do just about anything at all."[140]

The Star and the Director Clash

Just as Dean had clashed with directors and other actors in the past, he was at odds with them on *Giant*. The public urination was to be the first of many actions on Dean's part during the filming of *Giant* that much of the cast and crew thought bizarre.

Dean's behavior especially aggravated Stevens. Some sensed that the clash between Dean and Stevens was the classic conflict between a beginning actor and an established director. George Stevens was a veteran of the movies, having worked his way up from assis-

Actor Dennis Hopper appeared in all three of Dean's major pictures.

Dean and Giant *director George Stevens disagreed on the importance of the character of Jett Rink.*

tant cameraman in silent movies in the 1920s to screenwriter and finally becoming one of the most respected and most award-winning directors in Hollywood. It was not easy for him to deal with a young actor whose need to be the center of attention was so all-consuming. Stevens later said:

> Jimmy never understood that Jett Rink was only part of that film. He was never intended to be the central figure. I didn't want to focus on one character. Jimmy was so into that character he could only see it through Jett's eyes. He was as inflexible and as insensitive as Jett Rink as a performer. [141]

Throughout the filming of *Giant*, Dean complained that Stevens was abusing his talents. One of Dean's friends, the singer Eartha Kitt, later said, "He felt he was being sacrificed for Taylor and Rock Hudson, and he was not pleased about it. He blamed everything on the director. He said the picture was going too big in an artificial way."[142]

In essence, Dean and Stevens disagreed on how *Giant* fit into the larger universe of Dean's work. Dean saw Jett Rink as the maturing, gray-haired end product of the two younger characters he had previously played: Cal Trask in *Eden* and Jim Stark in *Rebel*. Biographer David Dalton, writing in *James Dean: American Icon*, notes

Despite feeling nervous about working with well-known stars like Rock Hudson and Elizabeth Taylor (pictured) in the film Giant, *Dean believed the experience would be good for his career.*

"Didn't Stevens realize [*Giant*] was part of a trilogy in which James Dean as prodigal son/rebel/victim would act out his [own] American tragedy?"[143]

As he had in *Rebel* Dean wanted to improvise, but Stevens wanted his actors to stick strictly to the script. Dalton notes that two philosophies of acting were on

> a collision course: the Method meets the System. Stevens' system allowed for as few surprises as possible. Every scene was meticulously worked out

with the actors and crew before rolling the film. Jimmy, who never played the same scene the same way twice, based his method of spontaneous combustion on its *unpredictability*.[144]

There was conflict with fellow actors as well. Rock Hudson found Dean difficult, if not strange, to work with. "Before coming on the set, he used to warm up like a fighter before a contest," Hudson recalled. "He never stepped into camera range without first jumping into the air with his knees up under his chin, or running at full speed around the set shrieking like a bird of prey."[145] Hudson also bluntly reported, "I didn't like him. Dean was hard to be around. [He was] always angry and full of contempt. He never smiled, was sulky, and had no manners."[146]

One of Dean's friends, Janette Miller, who later became a psychologist, said about Dean at this time,

> I felt that Hollywood exploited his dark side, his eccentricities and his psychological hang-ups. And it worked really

well for the studio. But he was angry at the people who were abusive or exploitative, and especially angry at those who challenged him.[147]

SYMPATHETIC ACTRESSES

While Dean did not get along with George Stevens and Rock Hudson, his relations with women on the picture were better. Elizabeth Taylor noticed Dean's misery and befriended him. Hudson later

Elizabeth Taylor, shown here with Dean on the set of Giant *was one of several actresses who befriended him.*

noted, "Dean was a very depressed person and Liz took to him in a most motherly fashion."[148]

Besides Taylor, another mother figure whom Dean attached himself to on *Giant* was Mercedes McCambridge, who played Hudson's older sister. McCambridge felt sorry for Dean. "I can't tell you how he wanted to be patted," she said later. "He was the runt in a litter of thoroughbreds, and you could feel the loneliness beating out of him."[149]

Another female cast member, Carroll Baker, tried to explain Dean's rude and shocking behavior both on and off the set: "He loved being a star," and would do anything for attention. "He wanted [attention] desperately, but it mattered so much that he almost had to treat it with contempt. He couldn't admit how much it meant to him."[150]

A PROFESSIONAL VIEW

During the filming of *Giant*, tensions between Dean and Stevens reached the point where a mediator was hired to talk to Dean. He was told the mediator, Dr. Emory Miller, was merely a "technical consultant," but Miller was actually a skilled professional psychologist. Since he was acting as a consultant and not in the role of a psychologist, Miller felt he was under no obligation of confidentiality. He later stated publicly that not only did Dean need an extraordinary amount of attention, but that he required that attention be on his own terms.

Dean's friend and biographer John Gilmore later said,

> The psychologist surmised that Dean had a "personality disorder. He responds to any criticism in a manner of defeat. Criticism reduces him to feelings of inferiority. He has rage in him, and he will rage against these criticisms and restrictions in a number of ways." [Dean and Cal Trask both suffer from] some unrequited love that literally runs him [Dean] ragged psychologically.[151]

After meeting with Dean, Miller concluded that part of Dean's troubles were based in a belief that he was in over his head:

> The problem as I see it, is that Jimmy Dean has bit off more than he can chew, and it's a problem he's trying to face repeatedly, with ever-increasing wear and tear psychologically. Whenever he is required to act a part that is not a direct extension of himself, and he knows this, he will be convinced he is failing—that it's all a disaster.[152]

Miller told George Stevens that Dean could not be swayed from the preoccupation with himself. "The difficulties as I see them," he said, "cannot be resolved." Miller's only suggestion was, "When he does something, praise him loudly—let him take the credit for whatever it is. Let Dean think he is the real hot dog."[153] Stevens rejected Miller's suggestion out of hand, saying, "No! The day I'm forced

James Dean (left), Rock Hudson (center), and Elizabeth Taylor (right) are shown at a luncheon before the filming of Giant.

to be subservient to an actor's whims is the day they can plant me in the daisies." [154]

Despite their differing opinions on the filming of *Giant*, Dean was later nominated for an Academy Award as best actor for his performance, as was Rock Hudson. Although neither actor won the award, Stevens won the Academy Award for best director.

"I'm Just Dog Tired"

As was his habit when he was in situations in which he felt insecure, Dean withdrew inside himself. He did the same when the cast and crew of *Giant* returned to the Warner Brothers studio in Burbank for their final work on the movie. Dean rented a cottage in the San

Fernando Valley, where he kept to himself. He told gossip columnist Dorothy Manners at this time,

> The trouble with me is that I'm just dog tired. Everybody hates me and thinks I'm a heel. They say I've gone Hollywood—but, honest, I'm just the same as when I didn't have a dime.

As I said, I'm just tired. I went into *Giant* immediately after a long hard schedule in *Rebel Without a Cause*. Maybe I'd better just go away.[155]

Meanwhile, Warner Brothers had big plans for Dean. The studio was drawing up a new contract offering Dean $1 million for nine movies over the next six years.

7 Death of a Giant

Upon completion of *Giant*, exhausted both physically and emotionally, Dean again sought release from his tensions and anxieties in fast sports car driving. Following his death in a crash, fans have kept the memory of James Dean alive through fan clubs all over the world.

A Spokesman for Safety

Near the end of filming *Giant*, Dean was asked to appear in a National Safety Council public service announcement about highway safety. In the spot, Dean made the point that racing was much safer than driving on the highways because "half the time you don't know what this guy's going to do, or that one."[156] The script called for him to conclude his remarks to teenagers by saying, "Drive safely, because the life you save may be your own." Dean, grinning mischievously, changed it to "Drive safely because the life you save may be mine."[157]

A few days later Jimmy traded in his Porsche Speedster for a new, dull gray

Dean purchased a new Porsche Spyder 550 that he intended to race once the filming of Giant *ended.*

Porsche Spyder 550. With a top speed of 120 miles per hour, it was considered one of the best new cars for racing. Dean told Rolf Weutherich, a mechanic at the dealership, "I'm going to buy the Spyder on the condition that you personally check it before each race and that you go with me to the races."[158] Weutherich agreed, on the orders of his employer.

After finishing work on *Giant*, Jimmy tested his new Porsche on the streets of Los Angeles. On one outing, speeding in the Hollywood hills with Eartha Kitt as passenger, Dean and the driver of another sports car began drag racing. The race ended when the other car sped off the road and up the side of a mountain. The driver was not hurt, but Dean told him, "You can't do the things I'm doing. I can flirt with death and come through—you can't."[159]

Kitt began to fear for Dean, feeling that he was purposely courting serious injury or death:

He didn't seem concerned about what had happened, or that someone —anyone, might've gotten killed. Going back, I said to him, "I don't like this car or these motorcycles. One of these cars is going to kill you." He laughed and told me to quit talking like that.[160]

A RETURN TO RACING

Dean was exhausted after finishing work on *Giant*, the third movie he had made in less than two years. As was his habit after completing a movie, he sought release in auto racing. He decided to enter a race in Salinas, where *East of Eden* had been filmed, about three hundred miles north of Los Angeles.

On the evening of Thursday, September 29, the day before leaving for the race, Dean test-drove his new sports car. With his friend and fellow race driver Bill Hickman as passenger, Dean sped up the coast highway near Santa Barbara, northwest of Los Angeles.

A California Highway Patrol officer tried to stop the speeding Porsche, but Dean easily left the police car behind. Having lost their pursuer, Dean and Hickman practiced techniques and strategies that Dean might need to use in the upcoming race. Finally, after practicing until nearly 11:00 P.M., they had a late-night dinner and then headed for an all-night party in Malibu.

Dean was up again at 7:30 A.M., after just a few hours of sleep, and dressed quickly in a pair of light blue trousers, a white T-shirt, brown shoes, and the red nylon windbreaker he had worn in *Rebel Without a Cause*. Dean considered it his lucky jacket and hoped it would help him win the Salinas race.

Dean was eager to get started for Salinas, but first he wanted to take his father for a ride in his new Porsche. Winton declined the ride. Instead, they went to a pizza parlor for a brief lunch. Afterward, Dean started for Salinas in the Spyder at about 1:30 P.M. with his mechanic Rolf Weutherich as his passenger.

Following behind Dean's Porsche in a Ford station wagon were Sanford Roth, a photographer who was going to take pictures of the race, and Bill Hickman.

A journey from Los Angeles to Salinas was then, before the completion of interstate highways, a trip of many hours, but Dean hoped to reach his destination by early evening in order to have a chance at a good night's rest.

At nearly 3:30 P.M., just south of Bakersfield, Dean was driving north on State Route 99 (now Interstate 5), when California Highway Patrol officer, Otie V. Hunter clocked him going sixty-five miles per hour in a forty-five miles per hour speed zone. Hunter stopped both cars and ticketed both Dean and Roth for speeding. The officer did not recognize Dean as a movie star. When he asked where Dean was going in such a hurry and Dean told him it was to a race in Salinas, he cautioned, "Take it easy, else you won't even make Salinas."[161] "I can't get her to run right at under eighty,"[162] Dean replied.

Dean then drove on, again followed by Roth and Hickman in the Ford, continuing on their way to Salinas. Dean began speeding again, still determined to make Salinas by early evening. On one stretch of road he sped as fast as 120 miles per hour. At another point, Dean, unwilling to let anyone get in his way, began to pass a car that was driving at the legal speed of 60 miles per hour. Pulling the Spyder into the left lane and accelerating until he was alongside the slower car, Dean saw a Pontiac heading straight for him. Rather than drop back behind the slower vehicle, Dean held his ground. The driver of the Pontiac, Clifford Hord, with his wife and young son and daughter in the car, avoided a head-on collision with Dean's sports car by cutting to his right and running off the side of the road into dirt and gravel. Without stopping to see if the Pontiac's occupants were injured, Dean continued toward Salinas.

Hord later estimated that Dean was driving at about 130 miles per hour at the time of their near head-on collision. Hord's shocked and frightened wife said "the two boys in the car [Dean and Weutherich] had been grinning from ear to ear as they watched [our Pontiac] veer off the road. [I will] never forget that smile and the blond hair snapping in the wind."[163]

Shortly afterward, at a brief stop at a gas station outside Bakersfield, Hickman cautioned Dean, "Be careful of the cars turning in front of you. The Spyder's hard to see because of the color and it being so low."[164]

Dean now headed west along Route 466 (now 46), a two-lane highway, toward the town of Cholame. Despite the oncoming darkness at dusk, he did not turn on his car's headlights.

One mile east of Cholame, squinting through his sunglasses as the setting sun shone in his eyes, Dean saw a Ford sedan traveling southeast on California Route 41. The road the Ford was travelling on would cross Dean's at a Y-shaped junction ahead. The driver of the Ford began to make a left turn onto 466, crossing into Dean's lane. "That guy's got to stop," Dean told Weutherich. "He'll see us."[165] They were to be James Dean's last words.

DEAN AND HIS FANS

Nine months after Dean's death there were more than four hundred fan clubs in America, Canada, Europe, and South America. In another year, they organized in Africa, Australia, and Japan. It was Dean's fans who best expressed what his movie performances and his life and death meant.

According to Paul Alexander in *Boulevard of Broken Dreams*, one fan, Joy Williams, said after seeing *Rebel Without a Cause*, "We were watching the intense, doomed performance of a dead youth, the myth of those who would wish to see themselves dead without dying. Dean was dead, predead, dead upon our discovery of him. His vivid presence projected a fathomless absence. It was thrilling."

A teenage girl explained Dean's appeal to her generation: "To us, Dean was a symbol of the fight to make a niche for ourselves in the world of adults. Something in us that is being sat on by convention and held down was, in Dean, free for all the world to see."

James Dean was killed instantly and his passenger was seriously injured when his Porsche collided with another car.

DEATH IN THE AFTERNOON

The driver of the Ford did not see the small gray car in the approaching dusk. He continued to make the turn that would cross right in front of Dean's car. Instead of applying his car's brakes in an attempt to avoid a collision, Dean floored the accelerator in hopes of swerving around the oncoming car.

The driver's side of the Porsche slammed into the passenger side of the Ford. In the next instant, Dean's car careened off the road and came to a halt close to a telephone pole. The Ford slid on down Route 466, eventually stopping.

Dean's car was totally smashed. Weutherich had been thrown from the Porsche upon impact and into a ditch. The collision had pinned Dean against the steering wheel and snapped his head back over the seat, breaking his neck and killing him.

Roth, driving the Ford wagon, pulled up to the scene of the accident. Minutes later an ambulance arrived to take Dean's body and the injured Weutherich to the War Memorial Hospital fifteen miles away in the town of Paso Robles. Weutherich was treated for multiple fractures, a broken jaw, and nearly lost a leg, but he eventually recovered. (Ironically,

Dean's funeral in Fairmount, Indiana, attracted over two thousand people.

twenty-six years later Weutherich would die in an auto accident in Germany.)

Remarkably, the other driver in the crash, Donald Turnupseed, 23, an electrical engineering student at what is today California Polytechnic University, received only a few cuts and bruises. Although he was in shock, his injuries did not require hospital treatment. At the crash scene, he kept repeating, "I never saw him. I never saw him."[166]

The investigation that followed established that Dean's excessive speed had been the cause of the accident.

A Funeral in Indiana

Winton Dean wanted his son to be buried beside Mildred Dean in Grant Memorial Park Cemetery in Marion, Indiana. However, Marcus Winslow, Dean's uncle, felt strongly about the burial being in Park Cemetery in Fairmount, and he won out. Winton accompanied his son's body on a plane back to Indiana.

A closed casket funeral service the following Saturday, October 8, at the Fairmount Friends Church was attended by over two thousand people. None of Dean's friends from Hollywood came to his funeral, with the exception of Henry Ginsberg, who was George Stevens's coproducer of *Giant*, and Steven Brooks, a Warner Brothers publicist.

When the two men from Hollywood were leaving after the funeral, Winslow asked, "When will all this die down?" One of the men replied, "Maybe in a couple of months."[167] Rudolph Valentino, one of the biggest stars of the silent films, had died at the age of thirty-one in 1926 at the height of his popularity, and his death resulted in mass hysteria among his female fans. Brooks agreed with Ginsberg that Dean would not be made into another Rudolph Valentino.

THE CULT OF JAMES DEAN

But the commotion did not die down. In the following months, it became clear that

Dean's short life and his untimely death had captured the imaginations of people everywhere. Reaction to his death started with obituaries circulated by wire services that appeared in newspapers throughout the world. Vicarious grief intensified after the release of *Rebel Without a Cause* about a month after Dean's death and again with the release of *Giant* about a year later.

James Dean's fans were determined to make sure that he would be remembered. As if he were still alive, they began sending several hundred letters a

Artist Kenneth Kendall sculpts a bust of James Dean. Dean's popularity reached cult status after his death.

week to Dean in care of Warner Brothers, then the mail swelled to seven thousand letters a month. Fans made pilgrimages to Dean's grave in Fairmount. They bought his photographs and sculptured busts of him. They ransacked places he had lived in search of mementos. Mostly, however, fans went to see his movies. Some fans saw *Rebel* twenty or thirty times or more.

Henry Ginsberg, commenting on the growing James Dean phenomenon, noted, "In sixteen months of acting, he left a more lasting impression on the public than many stars do in thirty years."[168]

Some cynics said Hollywood fanned the flames of the James Dean cult for its own profit. Observers of the movie industry noted that since the years of the silent films, Hollywood had been in the busi-

A teenage girl in the 1950s sits in her room surrounded by James Dean memorabilia.

DEAN AND A "DEATH WISH"

George Stevens disagreed with some who said that James Dean courted death. "Anyone who subscribes to this phony morbidity cult is doing an injustice to the memory of a great actor," Donald Spoto quotes him as saying in *Rebel: The Life and Legend of James Dean.* "I'm sure Jimmy would want to be judged solely on his talent and nothing else."

When rumors reached him that Dean had had a death wish, Stevens declared, "Morbid nonsense! Jimmy had no will to die. He was very much planning for the future."

In fact, Dean did have plans for his career as an actor. For one thing, he wanted to play both Hamlet and Billy the Kid.

Dean also had plans for his retirement, as he wrote in his journal in 1955, and is quoted in *James Dean: In His Own Words,* by Neil Grant, "I'm a small-town boy with small-town ideas. That's how I want to live. I intend some day to retire and farm."

ness of not only making movies but of manufacturing legends.

In the case of James Dean, Warner Brothers still had to market his two unreleased movies, *Rebel Without a Cause* and *Giant.* Frenzy over his death, some said, could help sell the pictures in which the studio had heavy financial investment. Furthermore, teenagers had become the 1950s' biggest new market targeted by media advertisers. For Hollywood and advertisers, the more news about Dean and his growing following, the better.

Dean had been the subject of only about a dozen Hollywood movie magazine articles before he died. After Dean's death, however, a flood of articles about him appeared in newspapers and fan magazines and overnight he became a cult figure. The authors of some articles insisted that Dean was still alive and included lengthy interviews that he allegedly had given them.

JAMES DEAN REMEMBERED

In the years since he died, many people have tried to gain insight into James Dean's character. William Mellor, who was the cinematographer on *Giant,* described Dean as "a small-town boy rocketed to success without warning, without preparation—an average young American still confused by a new life, not yet adjusted to fame, fortune, and fan mania."[169] Dean

James Dean is remembered for having effectively portrayed the struggles and frustrations of teenagers everywhere.

had admitted as much to himself, writing in his journal in 1955, "I've got a lot of growing up to do yet. I've got to be given time to master the art of handling Hollywood—to learn what to say and what not to say."[170] Forty years later composer Leonard Rosenman said,

> I really think Jimmy had no idea in the world who or what he was. Obviously he identified with the three ma-

jor roles he had, but I think they were given to him because he was those roles, or in some ways they were created for him—and it all had to do with confusion!"[171]

Dean never thought highly of himself, according to biographer David Dalton, who quotes him as saying, "Why should I be loved? I'm . . . a nothing, a no good." Dalton says,

He could never forget he was an orphan, nor was he about to let us forget it either. In all his films, Jimmy played orphans—either metaphorical or actual. The foundling adopted by uncomprehending human parents, the heroic orphan of mythology.[172]

In the fall of 1957 Warner Brothers released a documentary, *The James Dean Story*. In London, the *Observer* said, "In James Dean, a generation mourns its own demise. He has become the symbol of frustrated youth, of mixed-up kiddery, revolt and loneliness."[173] Thus, the legend of James Dean spread throughout the world. Hundreds of his fans come each year to attend a James Dean memorial weekend in Fairmount.

Many teenagers looked at themselves differently after seeing *Rebel Without a Cause*, as Dalton notes in his biography of Dean:

Rebel overthrew the notion that in order to grow up you must somehow *become* your parents. On the contrary, to accept yourself excluded any such compromise with conformity. Adolescence was no longer a frustrating phase on the way to the privileges of adulthood, but *the* desirable state, and James Dean's performance radiated the ironic defiance of the underdog. The Teen Dream was born, and Jimmy was speaking for all of us.

James Dean was the shapeshifter and matrix of adolescence, literally its masterpiece, in the original sense of the master mold from which statues are cast. After Jimmy, adolescence began to seem an end in itself, the that-beyond-which nothing would, even if possible, be desirable. By determining that we would never have to "grow up," he made what had heretofore been seen as a "passing phase" into a phenomenon. He proved that growing up was impossible. It just couldn't be done. Consistently playing the outsider in all of his films, Jimmy formed a bond with hostility.[174]

Another writer, Mike Wilmington, wrote in *High Times* that Dean became more than someone with whom teens could identify:

They [teenagers] saw in Dean an image of themselves: purified, idealized, and spread triumphantly across a Technicolor CinemaScope screen. But there was something more, too. Who would have predicted that their loyalty to this tyro actor in bluejeans would so far outstrip and survive his death? Would survive their youth, too—and the times that engendered them—and would, in turn, grip the next wave of youth, and the wave after that . . . give them a touchstone, an idol and, in the end, make James Dean something he always sought—in his confused, murderously determined way—to be a symbol. Immortal.[175]

Two of Dean's friends may have come the closest to understanding him. Dizzy

IN MEMORY OF JAMES DEAN

THE FAIRMOUNT NEWS

Volume LXXX   Fairmount, Grant County, Indiana   SPECIAL EDITION

James Dean Killed As Result Of California Car Accident

FAIRMOUNT IS STUNNED TO LEARN OF TRAGEDY WHICH CLAIMED NATIVE SON; HEADON COLLISION NEAR INTERSECTION CAUSES FATALITY FRIDAY

Special

JAMES DEAN'S "EDEN" PROVES HIGH TALENT OF FAIRMOUNT ACTOR

... a Student at U.C.L.A.

James Dean

Photo by Curtis Bernard, Santa Monica, Calif.

Last Rites Will Be Held Here Saturday

Dr. James A. DeWeerd, Rev. Xen Harvey To Conduct

Basketball Star

Hockett Studio

DEATH OF JAMES DEAN, FAIRMOUNT HIGH ALUMNI CASTS A PALL OF SADNESS OVER STUDENT BODY

$105,000 ESTATE LEFT BY ACTOR JIMMY DEAN

James Dean's death made headlines in his hometown of Fairmount and around the nation.

Sheridan said, "He was like a bottomless well. No matter how much anyone or everyone offered, no love was enough."[176] And Leonard Rosenman said, "He was doing everything for one person—his father. And his father never took the re-

motest interest."[177] It was no wonder that Dean could identify so well with Cal Trask in *East of Eden*, a character who tried so hard to get love from an unloving father.

Because he was so empty and felt worthless, Jimmy had wanted to be the best.

Prophetically, he wrote his own epitaph when in high school he wrote, "If a man can bridge the gap between life and death . . . If he can live on after he's died, then maybe he was a great man. To me, the only success, the only greatness, is immortality."[178]

James Dean achieved what he sought. In his expressions of youthful frustrations and anxieties both on and off the screen, and in his early and tragic death, he achieved at least a portion of what was so important to him.

Notes

Introduction: Rebel with a Cause

1. Quoted in American Movie Classics, *James Dean: A Portrait*, documentary, October 12, 1999.

2. Quoted in John Gilmore, *Live Fast—Die Young: Remembering the Short Life of James Dean*. New York: Thunder's Mouth, 1997, p. xiii.

Chapter 1: Orphan with a Father

3. Quoted in Val Holley, *James Dean: The Biography*. New York: St. Martin's, 1995, p. 17.

4. Quoted in David Dalton, *James Dean: The Mutant King*. San Francisco: Straight Arrow Books, 1974, p. 4.

5. Quoted in Gilmore, *Live Fast*, p. 34.

6. Quoted in Paul Alexander, *Boulevard of Broken Dreams: The Life, Times, and Legend of James Dean*. New York: Viking, 1994, p. 18.

7. Gilmore, *Live Fast*, p. 35.

8. Quoted in Gilmore, *Live Fast*, p. 35.

9. Gilmore, *Live Fast*, p. 35.

10. Quoted in Holley, *James Dean*, p. 18.

11. Quoted in Holley, *James Dean*, p. 18.

12. Quoted in John Howlett, *James Dean: A Biography*. London: Plexus, 1997, p. 13.

13. Quoted in Dalton, *James Dean: The Mutant King*, p. 5.

14. Quoted in Emma Woolen Dean, "James Dean—the Boy I Loved," *Photoplay*, March 1956, p. 84.

15. Quoted in Alexander, *Boulevard of Broken Dreams*, p. 26.

16. Quoted in Holley, *James Dean*, pp. 18–19.

Chapter 2: A Troubled Young Loner

17. Quoted in Howlett, *James Dean*, p. 16.

18. Quoted in David Dalton, *James Dean: American Icon*. New York: St. Martin's, 1984, p. 16.

19. Quoted in Dalton, *James Dean: The Mutant King*, p. 32.

20. Quoted in Donald Spoto, *Rebel: The Life and Legend of James Dean*. New York: HarperCollins, 1996, p. 34.

21. Quoted in Spoto, *Rebel*, p. 51.

22. Quoted in Holley, *James Dean*, p. 21.

23. Quoted in Neil Grant, *James Dean: In His Own Words*. New York: Crescent, 1991, p. 10.

24. Quoted in Grant, *James Dean*, p. 10.

25. Quoted in Joe Hyams, *James Dean: Little Boy Lost*. New York: Warner Books, 1992, p. 15.

26. Quoted in Alexander, *Boulevard of Broken Dreams*, p. 42.

27. Quoted in Hyams, *James Dean*, p. 18.

28. Quoted in Holley, *James Dean*, p. 16.

29. Quoted in Holley, *James Dean*, p. 16.

30. Quoted in Spoto, *Rebel*, p. 33.

31. Quoted in Spoto, *Rebel*, pp. 33–34.

32. Quoted in Dalton, *James Dean: American Icon*, p. 16.

33. Quoted in Spoto, *Rebel*, p. 36.

34. Quoted in Holley, *James Dean*, p. 23.

35. Quoted in Spoto, *Rebel*, p. 37.

36. Quoted in Alexander, *Boulevard of Broken Dreams*, p. 43.

37. Quoted in Hyams, *James Dean*, p. 19.

38. Quoted in Gilmore, *Live Fast*, p. 46.

39. Quoted in Hyams, *James Dean*, p. 20.

40. Quoted in Holley, *James Dean*, p. 26.

41. Quoted in Howlett, *James Dean*, p. 19.

42. Quoted in Holley, *James Dean*, p. 26.

43. Quoted in Dalton: *James Dean: The Mutant King*, p. 36.

Chapter 3: Experiments with Acting and Life

44. Quoted in Gilmore, *Live Fast*, p. 49.
45. Quoted in Gilmore, *Live Fast*, p. 51.
46. Quoted in Gilmore, *Live Fast*, p. 50.
47. Quoted in Howlett, *James Dean*, pp. 23–24.
48. Quoted in Howlett, *James Dean*, p. 24.
49. Quoted in Grant, *James Dean*, p. 13.
50. Quoted in Spoto, *Rebel*, p. 76.
51. Quoted in Gilmore, *Live Fast*, p. 57.
52. Quoted in Grant, *James Dean*, p. 8.
53. Quoted in Grant, *James Dean*, p. 18.
54. Quoted in Spoto, *Rebel*, p. 74.
55. Quoted in Gilmore, *Live Fast*, p. 65.
56. Quoted in Gilmore, *Live Fast*, p. 61.
57. Quoted in Spoto, *Rebel*, p. 86.
58. Quoted in Spoto, *Rebel*, pp. 84–85.
59. Quoted in Gilmore, *Live Fast*, p. 60.
60. Quoted in Gilmore, *Live Fast*, p. 65.
61. Gilmore, *Live Fast*, p. 6.
62. Quoted in Gilmore, *Live Fast*, p. 69.
63. Quoted in Gilmore, *Live Fast*, pp. 62–63.
64. Gilmore, *Live Fast*, p. 66.
65. Quoted in Grant, *James Dean*, p. 18.
66. Quoted in Spoto, *Rebel*, p. 81.
67. Quoted in Spoto, *Rebel*, p. 87.
68. Quoted in Grant, *James Dean*, p. 15.

Chapter 4: A New Kind of Teenage Actor

69. Quoted in Spoto, *Rebel*, p. 91.
70. Quoted in Grant, *James Dean*, p. 20.
71. Quoted in Grant, *James Dean*, p. 17.
72. Quoted in Gilmore, *Live Fast*, p. 18.
73. Quoted in Gilmore, *Live Fast*, p. 18.
74. Quoted in Howlett, *James Dean*, p. 43.
75. Quoted in Hyams, *James Dean*, pp. 45–46.
76. Quoted in Gilmore, *Live Fast*, p. 73.
77. Quoted in Gilmore, *Live Fast*, p. 75.
78. Quoted in Gilmore, *Live Fast*, p. 87.
79. Quoted in Spoto, *Rebel*, p. 99.
80. Quoted in Holley, *James Dean*, p. 128.
81. Quoted in Holley, *James Dean*, p. 128.
82. Quoted in Holley, *James Dean*, p. 132.
83. Quoted in Gilmore, *Live Fast*, p. 16.
84. Quoted in Hyams, *James Dean*, p. 64.
85. Quoted in Holley, *James Dean*, p. 133.
86. Quoted in Howlett, *James Dean*, p. 48.
87. Quoted in Spoto, *Rebel*, p. 118.
88. Quoted in Gilmore, *Live Fast*, p. 84.
89. Quoted in Spoto, *Rebel*, p. 119.
90. Quoted in Hyams, *James Dean*, p. 70.
91. Quoted in Hyams, *James Dean*, pp. 68–69.
92. Quoted in Gilmore, *Live Fast*, p. 133.
93. Quoted in Gilmore, *Live Fast*, p. 134.
94. Quoted in Holley, *James Dean*, p. 7.

Chapter 5: Success but No Peace

95. Quoted in Alexander, *Boulevard of Broken Dreams*, p. 154.
96. Quoted in Holley, *James Dean*, p. 191.
97. Gilmore, *Live Fast*, p. 76.
98. Quoted in Dalton, *James Dean*, p. 54.
99. Quoted in Holley, *James Dean*, p. 191.
100. Quoted in Gilmore, *Live Fast*, p. 136.
101. Quoted in Holley, *James Dean*, pp. 196–197.
102. Gilmore, *Live Fast*, p. 146.
103. Quoted in Dalton, *James Dean*, p. 46.
104. Quoted in Alexander, *Boulevard of Broken Dreams*, p. 161.
105. Quoted in Spoto, *Rebel*, p. 164.
106. Quoted in Holley, *James Dean*, p. 7.
107. Quoted in Holley, *James Dean*, p. 198.
108. Quoted in Grant, *James Dean*, p. 25.
109. Quoted in Holley, *James Dean*, p. 201.

110. Quoted in Holley, *James Dean*, p. 201.

111. Quoted in Holley, *James Dean*, p. 199.

112. Quoted in Hyams, *James Dean*, p. 149.

113. Quoted in Gilmore, *Live Fast*, p. 163.

114. Gilmore, *Live Fast*, p. 163.

115. Quoted in Dalton, *James Dean: American Icon*, p. 20.

116. Quoted in Alexander, *Boulevard of Broken Dreams*, p. 188.

117. Quoted in Dalton, *James Dean*, p. 57.

118. Quoted in Dalton, *James Dean*, pp. 59–60.

119. Quoted in Grant, *James Dean*, p. 47.

Chapter 6: Personification of a Teenage Rebel

120. Quoted in Spoto, *Rebel*, p. 212.

121. Quoted in Spoto, *Rebel*, p. 212.

122. Quoted in Grant, *James Dean*, p. 42.

123. Quoted in Dalton, *James Dean: American Icon*, p. 96.

124. Quoted in Dalton, *James Dean: American Icon*, p. 77.

125. Quoted in Grant, *James Dean*, p. 41.

126. Quoted in Howlett, *James Dean*, p. 112.

127. Quoted in Grant, *James Dean*, p. 39.

128. Quoted in Dalton, *James Dean: American Icon*, p. 105.

129. Quoted in Grant, *James Dean*, p. 44.

130. Quoted in Grant, *James Dean*, p. 47.

131. Quoted in Howlett, *James Dean*, p. 96.

132. Quoted in Grant, *James Dean*, p. 59.

133. Quoted in American Movie Classics, *James Dean*.

134. Quoted in Howlett, *James Dean*, p. 113.

135. Quoted in Hyams, *James Dean*, p. 217.

136. Quoted in Grant, *James Dean*, p. 38.

137. Quoted in Hyams, *James Dean*, p. 218.

138. Quoted in Hyams, *James Dean*, p. 218.

139. Quoted in Hyams, *James Dean*, p. 220.

140. Quoted in Hyams, *James Dean*, p. 220.

141. Quoted in Dalton, *James Dean: American Icon*, p. 131.

142. Quoted in Dalton, *James Dean: American Icon*, p. 123.

143. Dalton, *James Dean: American Icon*, p. 123.

144. Dalton, *James Dean: American Icon*, p. 139.

145. Quoted in Dalton, *James Dean: American Icon*, p. 134.

146. Quoted in Hyams, *James Dean*, p. 234.

147. Quoted in Hyams, *James Dean*, p. 225.

148. Quoted in Hyams, *James Dean*, p. 223.

149. Quoted in Hyams, *James Dean*, p. 222.

150. Quoted in Spoto, *Rebel*, p. 235.

151. Gilmore, *Live Fast*, p. 227.

152. Quoted in Gilmore, *Live Fast*, p. 228.

153. Quoted in Gilmore, *Live Fast*, p. 228.

154. Quoted in Gilmore, *Live Fast*, p. 228.

155. Quoted in Alexander, *Boulevard of Broken Dreams*, p. 218.

Chapter 7: Death of a Giant

156. Quoted in Holley, *James Dean*, p. 277.

157. Quoted in American Movie Classics, *James Dean*.

158. Quoted in Hyams, *James Dean*, pp. 233–34.

159. Quoted in Gilmore, *Live Fast*, p. 216.

160. Quoted in Gilmore, *Live Fast*, p. 216.

161. Quoted in Howlett, *James Dean*, p. 143.

162. Quoted in Howlett, *James Dean*, p. 143.

163. Quoted in Warren Newton Beath, *The Death of James Dean*. New York: Grove, 1986, p. 45.

164. Quoted in Hyams, *James Dean*, p. 245.

165. Quoted in Alexander, *Boulevard of Broken Dreams*, p. 242.

166. Quoted in Alexander, *Boulevard of Broken Dreams*, p. 248.

167. Quoted in Alexander, *Boulevard of Broken Dreams*, p. 258.

168. Quoted in Spoto, *Rebel*, p. 251.

169. Quoted in Spoto, *Rebel*, p. 235.

170. Quoted in Grant, *James Dean*, p. 61.

171. Quoted in Spoto, *Rebel*, p. 235.

172. Dalton, *James Dean: American Icon*, p. 219.

173. Quoted in Alexander, *Boulevard of Broken Dreams*, pp. 280–81.

174. Dalton, *James Dean: American Icon*, pp. 237–47.

175. Quoted in Dalton, *James Dean: American Icon*, p. 218.

176. Quoted in Spoto, *Rebel*, p. 118.

177. Quoted in Spoto, *Rebel*, p. 210.

178. Quoted in Grant, *James Dean*, p. 62.

Filmography

Motion Pictures

1951 *Fixed Bayonets*

1952 *Sailor Beware*

      Has Anybody Seen My Gal?

1953 *Trouble Along the Way*

1955 *East of Eden*

      Rebel Without a Cause

1956 *Giant*

Television

1951 "Hill Number One," *Family Theater*

1952 "Sleeping Dogs," *The Web*

      "Ten Thousand Horses Singing," *Studio One*

      "The Foggy, Foggy Dew," *Lux Video Theater*

      "Prologue to Glory," *U.S. Steel Hour*

      "Abraham Lincoln," *Studio One*

      "Forgotten Children," *Hallmark Hall of Fame*

1953 "Hound of Heaven," *Kate Smith Show*

      "The Case of the Watchful Dog," *Treasury Men in Action*

      "The Capture of Jesse James," *You Are There*

      "No Room," *Danger*

      "The Case of the Sawed-Off Shotgun," *Treasury Men in Action*

      "Something for an Empty Briefcase," *Campbell Soundstage*

      "Sentence of Death," *Studio One Summer Theater*

      "Death Is My Neighbor," *Danger*

      "The Evil Within," *Tales of Tomorrow*

      "The Big Story"

      "Glory in the Flower," *Omnibus*

      "Keep Our Honor Bright," *Kraft Television Theater*

      "Life Sentence," *Campbell Soundstage*

      "A Long Time Till Dawn," *Kraft Television Theater*

      "The Bells of Cockaigne," *Armstrong Circle Theater*

      "Harvest," *Robert Montgomery Presents the Johnson's Wax Program*

1954 "The Little Woman," *Danger*

      "Run Like a Thief," *Philco TV Playhouse*

      "Padlocks," *Danger*

      "I'm a Fool," *General Electric Theater*

      "The Dark, Dark Hour," *General Electric Theater*

      "The Thief," *U.S. Steel Hour*

1955 "The Unlighted Road," *Schlitz Playhouse of Stars*

Plays (On Broadway)

1952 *See the Jaguar*

1954 *The Immoralist*

Plays (Off Broadway)

1952 *The Metamorphosis*

1953 *The Scarecrow*

1954 *Women of Trachis*

Films About or Inspired by James Dean

1957 *The James Dean Story*

1976 *James Dean: The First American Teenager*

James Dean: The Legend

1977 *September 30, 1955*

1982 *Come Back to the Five and Dime, Jimmy Dean, Jimmy Dean*

1996 *James Dean: A Portrait*

1998 *James Dean: Live Fast, Die Young*

For Further Reading

David Dalton, *James Dean: American Icon.* New York: St. Martin's, 1984. A brief biography of Dean as a cult hero. Contains more photos than in any other Dean biography. An adult biography suitable for younger readers.

Thomas Doherty, *Teenagers and Teenpics: The Juvenilazation of American Movies in the 1950s.* Winchester, MA: Unwin Hyman, 1988. Assesses movies about teens in the 1950s.

Venable Herndon, *James Dean: A Short Life.* New York: Signet/NAL, 1975. A standard biography of James Dean that accentuates the positive aspects of his character. An adult book suitable for young adults.

Randall Riese, *The Unabridged James Dean: His Life and Legacy from A to Z.* Chicago: Contemporary Books, 1991. A biography of James Dean that concentrates on the most widely reported aspects of the actor's life. An adult book about Dean that is suitable for young adults.

Allan Schroeder, *James Dean.* New York: Chelsea House, 1994. A biography of Dean written for young adults, by the author of numerous books about famous people.

Website

James Dean Home Page: www.jamesdean. com/then/fest/html. This website contains a wealth of information on James Dean and his fans' activities to keep his legend alive.

Works Consulted

Books

Paul Alexander, *Boulevard of Broken Dreams: The Life, Times, and Legend of James Dean*. New York: Viking, 1994. The author, a former *Time* magazine reporter describes many of Dean's personality conflicts. Contains some never-before-published photos. This is an adult book and is not suitable for young readers.

Warren Newton Beath, *The Death of James Dean*. New York: Grove, 1986. The most comprehensive reporting on Dean's final days and his death, from police and other interviews. Contains photos and a diagram of the fatal auto crash. An adult book suitable for young adult readers.

David Dalton, *James Dean: The Mutant King*. San Francisco: Straight Arrow Books, 1974. The book is based on the author's research and interviews with James Dean's family, friends, and coworkers, and it assesses the actor's significance twenty years after his death. An adult book suitable for young adults.

John Gilmore, *Live Fast—Die Young: Remembering the Short Life of James Dean*. New York: Thunder's Mouth, 1997. The only biography of Dean written by a close friend. The former actor, now a screenwriter, director, and author, writes a graphic account of Dean's personal life, based on letters, diaries, private reminiscences, and interviews with those who knew the actor. An adult book not suitable for young readers.

Neil Grant, *James Dean: In His Own Words*. New York: Crescent, 1991. A British author of social history books, Grant compiles quotes from Dean's letters, notebooks, and conversations in an oversized book with a brief summary of Dean's life and career, interspersed with many photos. Suitable for young adult readers.

Val Holley, *James Dean: The Biography*. New York: St. Martin's, 1995. A writer of magazine articles on Dean and other celebrities, Holley describes Dean's life and career with a special focus on his early life and training on the stage and in television. A comprehensive biography written for adults but suitable for young adult readers.

John Howlett, *James Dean: A Biography*. London: Plexus, 1997. The British author draws on previous books about Dean and on new interviews to write a comprehensive biography of the actor. This book attempts to assess Dean's status today as a cult hero. An adult biography suitable for young adult readers.

Joe Hyams, *James Dean: Little Boy Lost*. New York: Warner Books, 1992. A biography focusing on Dean's attempts to adjust to the pressures and obligations that went with his fame as an actor.

Donald Spoto, *Rebel: The Life and Legend of James Dean*. New York: HarperCollins, 1996. The author of other biographies of film stars writes a revealing biography of James Dean's personal life based on new research and interviews and assesses the actor's status as a cult figure. An adult book also suitable for young adults.

Periodicals

Jeanine Basinger, "Remembering *Rebel*," *American Movie Classics Magazine*, October 1999.

Susan Bluttman, "Rediscovering James Dean: The TV Legacy," *Emmy*, October 1990.

Jim Cook, "Jimmy Dean Is Not Dead," *Motion Picture*, May 1956.

Emma Woolen Dean, "James Dean—the Boy I Loved," *Photoplay*, March 1956.

Television

James Dean: A Portrait, American Movie classics Documentary, October 12, 1999.

Index

Picture Credits

Cover photo: Stills/Retna, LTD.

AP, 38, 55, 85

Bettmann/Corbis, 12, 13, 16, 20, 29, 31, 50, 75, 77, 79, 83, 84, 86, 90

Corbis/Bettmann, 22

Hulton-Deutsch Collection/Corbis-Bettmann, 45

John Springer/Corbis-Bettmann, 34, 67

UPI/Corbis-Bettmann, 10

FPG Inc., 43, 60, 61

Sanford Roth/FPG Inc., 26

Photofest, 15, 17, 23, 25, 35, 37, 39, 40, 47, 49, 51, 52, 56, 58, 59, 63, 64, 65, 68, 69, 72, 73, 74, 88

About the Author

Walter Oleksy writes novels and nonfiction books for preteens, young adults, and adults.

His novels include *If I'm Lost, How Come I Found You?*; *Bug Scanner and the Computer Mystery*; *The Pirates of Deadman's Cay*; *Land of the Lost Dinosaurs*; and the four-book young adult series *The Guardians*: *Up from Nowhere*, *One-Way Trip*, *Easy Way Out*, and *The Final Act*.

His nonfiction books include *Lincoln's Unknown Private Life*, *The Information Revolution*, *Hispanic-American Scientists*, *The Philippines*, *Mikhail Gorbachev: A Leader for Soviet Change*, *The Black Plague*, *American Military Leaders of World War II*, *Careers in the Animal Kingdom*, and, for Lucent Books, biographies of *Christopher Reeve* and *Princess Diana*.

Oleksy lives in a Chicago suburb with his dog, Max, a black lab-shepherd mix who likes to talk and take walks in the woods with his master.

A Note to Parents

DK READERS is a compelling program for beginning readers, designed in conjunction with leading literacy experts, including Dr. Linda Gambrell, Director of the School of Education at Clemson University. Dr. Gambrell has served on the Board of Directors of the International Reading Association and as President of the National Reading Conference.

Beautiful illustrations and superb full-color photographs combine with engaging, easy-to-read stories to offer a fresh approach to each subject in the series. Each DK READER is guaranteed to capture a child's interest while developing his or her reading skills, general knowledge, and love of reading.

The five levels of DK READERS are aimed at different reading abilities, enabling you to choose the books that are exactly right for your child:
Pre-level 1: Learning to read
Level 1: Beginning to read
Level 2: Beginning to read alone
Level 3: Reading alone
Level 4: Proficient readers

The "normal" age at which a child begins to read can be anywhere from three to eight years old, so these levels are only a general guideline.

No matter which level you select, you can be sure that you are helping your child learn to read, then read to learn!

LONDON, NEW YORK, MUNICH,
MELBOURNE, AND DELHI

Project Editors Anna Lofthouse
and Caryn Jenner
Series Editor Deborah Lock
Senior Art Editor Cheryl Telfer
Project Art Editor Jacqueline Gooden
Art Editor Nicky Liddiard
U.S. Editor Elizabeth Hester
DTP Designer Almudena Díaz
Production Shivani Pandey
Jacket Designer Chris Drew
Indexer Lynn Bresler
Reading Consultant
Linda Gambrell, Ph.D.

First American Edition, 2003
06 07 08 09 10 9 8 7 6
Published in the United States by DK Publishing, Inc.
375 Hudson Street, New York, New York 10014

Published in Great Britain by Dorling Kindersley Limited

Library of Congress Cataloging-in-Publication Data
Hayden, Kate.
   Amazing buildings / by Kate Hayden.
   --1st American ed.
     p. cm. -- (Dorling Kindersley readers)
   Summary: Showcases such unusual buildings as Stadium Australia,
the Eiffel Tower, and the Roman Colosseum.
   ISBN-13: 978-0-7894-9308-8   ISBN-10: 0-7894-9308-X
   ISBN-13: 978-0-7894-9220-3   ISBN-10: 0-7894-9220-2 (pbk.)
   1. Buildings--Juvenile literature. 2. Architecture--Juvenile literature.
[1.Buildings. 2.Architecture.] I. Title. II. Dorling Kindersley readers.
NA2555. H39 2003
720'.9--dc21   2002073391

Color reproduction by Colourscan, Singapore
Printed and bound in China by L Rex Printing Co., Ltd.

The publisher would like to thank the following for their kind permission
to reproduce their images: c=center, a=above, b=below, l=left, r=right.
   2: Corbis: tr, br; 3: Corbis; 4: Getty Images/Image Bank bl;
   5: ImageState tl, tr, cl, b; 6-7: Still Pictures; 11: Corbis t; 12: Corbis br;
   13: Getty Images/Telegraph; 14-15: James Davis Travel Photography;
   15: Corbis tr, Hutchison Library/John Hatt bc; 16: Corbis; 17: Corbis;
   18: Corbis; 19: Getty Images/Image Bank br; 20: Getty Images/Stone;
   21: Getty Images/Stone; 22: Corbis bl. 22-23: Powerstock Photolibrary;
   24-5: Corbis; 25: ImageState c, Zefa tr; 26-7: Katz/FSP; 27: Agence
   France Presse tr; 28: Apex Photo Agency/Simon Burt tl; 28-29:
alamy.com b, Zefa Picture Library t; 29: Apex Photo Agency/Simon cl;
   30-31: NASA t; 32: Corbis tl, tr, cl, cr; 33: Corbis
   All other images © Dorling Kindersley
   For further information see: www.dkimages.com

Discover more at

www.dk.com

READERS

BEGINNING TO READ ALONE
2

Amazing Buildings

Written by Kate Hayden

DK Publishing, Inc.

Imagine a building–
an amazing building.
Does your building stand up tall?
Or does it spread out **wide?**
Is your building new,
with lots of shiny windows?
Or is it old and made of stone?
Do you know how
buildings are made?

1) An architect draws plans and makes models to show what a building will look like.

2) Construction workers lay sturdy foundations in the ground.

3) They build the walls, leaving gaps for the windows and doors.

4) The roof is added, and then glass is put in the windows.

A big city like this has
all kinds of buildings.
There are tall buildings,
wide buildings, office buildings,
apartment buildings, and more.

There are weird and wonderful
buildings all over the world.
They are built to be both
useful and fun to look at.

The pyramids in Egypt
were built over 4,000 years ago.
These monuments were made
as burial sites for
Egyptian kings and
their treasure.

To build the pyramids, workers had to drag heavy stones up a ramp, one by one.

Many hands
It took 4,000 men twenty years to build the biggest pyramid.

The pyramids were built to last for a long time.

The Ancient Romans built
a massive stadium called
the Colosseum.
The Romans were the first to
use concrete
to make
buildings.

The Colosseum was oval-shaped and seated up to 50,000 people. The Romans loved to watch trained fighters, called gladiators, battle each other. Cheers and boos from the crowd made echoes all around the stadium.

This fairy-tale castle, perched on a craggy hilltop in Germany, is called Neuschwanstein (NOY-shvan-stine). Earlier castles were built to protect the people inside, who could spy on approaching enemies from the tall towers. But Neuschwanstein was built just to look beautiful.

A Disney castle
Does this castle look familiar? Cinderella's castle in Disneyland is modeled after Neuschwanstein Castle.

One of the world's biggest palaces
is at Versailles (ver-SY) in France.
It has over 2,000 windows,
1,200 fireplaces and 67 staircases.
There is also a Hall of Mirrors
at Versailles.

When the palace
was built 300 years ago,
mirrors were very rare.
Visitors were amazed
to see their reflections.

Fit for a King
The King's bedroom
was at the center
of the palace.
Louis XIV even
signed papers in bed!

The Eiffel Tower in Paris, France, is made of iron.

It was the tallest building in the world when it was built in 1889.

In those days it was unusual to make buildings out of metal. Since then, metal has been used to make buildings taller and **taller.**

Extra strength
The criss-cross pattern of the metal bars gives the Eiffel Tower extra strength and stability.

The tallest buildings of all
are called skyscrapers because
they seem to touch the sky.
The two Petronas Towers in
Malaysia are the tallest skyscrapers in
the world, at 1,483 feet (452 meters).
Each tower has 88 floors.
Visitors can walk
from one building
to the other on
the Skybridge.

It takes a whole
month to clean
all the windows
on one tower!

Some buildings have big, round roofs called domes.

The dome on Florence Cathedral in Italy was difficult to build. Builders had to make another dome inside the cathedral to support the huge outer dome. Workers walked through passages between the inner and outer domes.

The domes on
St. Basil's Cathedral
in Russia are called
onion domes.

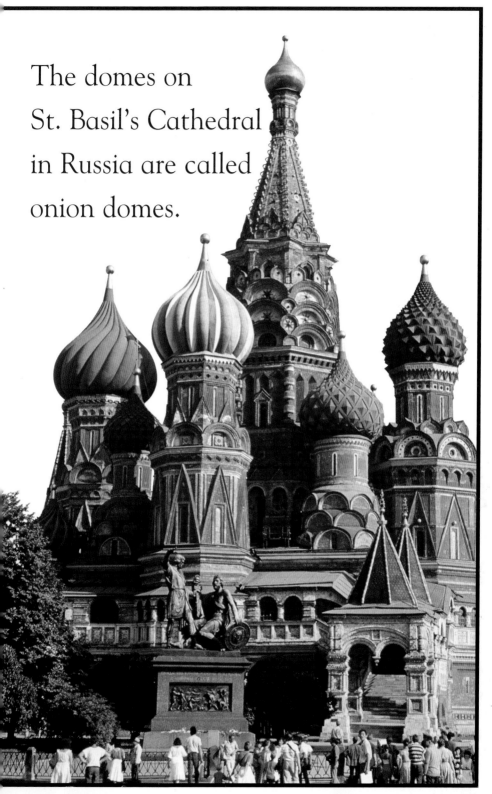

Have you ever seen a building
in the shape of a ball?
The round building in this picture
is called Spaceship Earth.
It is at the Epcot Center
theme park in Florida.
Over 11,000 triangles cover
the surface to make it look
perfectly round and white–like
a huge golf ball!

More curves

This hotel in Dubai was
designed to look like a
wave. It has 600 rooms
for guests—all with
ocean views!

Think of the amazing shapes
of other modern buildings.
What do these buildings
look like to you?

The Sydney Opera House
in Australia looks like
the billowing sails
of a sailing boat.

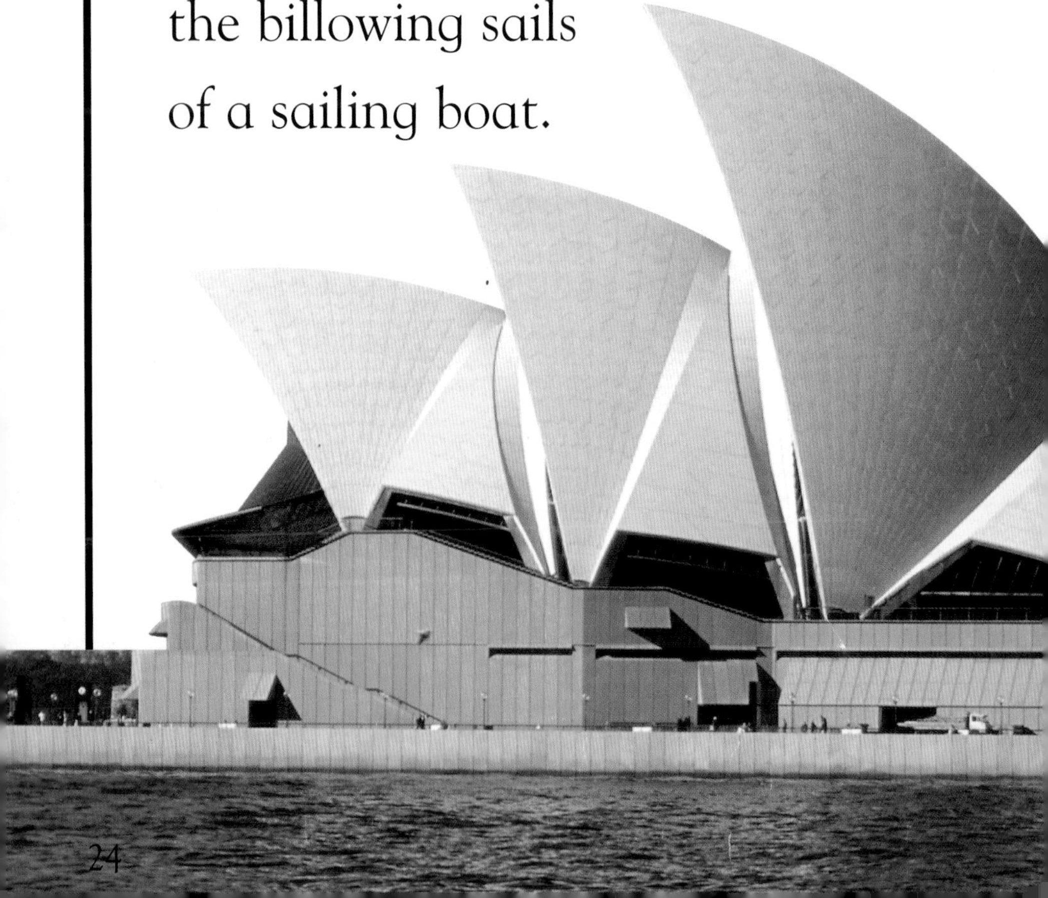

The Guggenheim Museum in Spain may remind you of a large ship.

A gleaming roof
The roof of the Sydney Opera House is covered by over one million ceramic tiles.

Look at this huge stadium.
Stadium Australia was built for
the games of the 2000 Olympics.
It was designed to be friendly
to the environment.
This means it uses less electricity
for lights and air conditioning.

Olympics
New stadiums are often built for special events, such as the Olympic Games.

The stadium has big tanks to collect rainwater that falls on the roof. The rainwater is recycled to water the field or even to flush the toilets!

Where can you grow bananas indoors? In a giant greenhouse!

At the Eden Project in England, the latest technology is used to create habitats from around the world.

Even when it's cold and dry outside, the weather is hot and damp inside the Humid Tropics Biome.

Jungle plants grow as if they are in the middle of a rain forest.

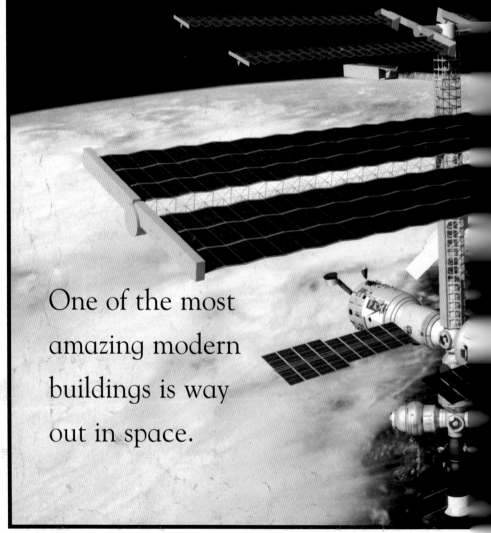

One of the most
amazing modern
buildings is way
out in space.

All of the parts for the International Space Station come from Earth, on board the Space Shuttle. Who knows what other amazing buildings may be built in the future?

More building facts

A moat surrounds many castles, such as Raglan Castle in Great Britain. A moat is a ditch filled with water to keep enemies out.

The Ice Hotel in Canada is rebuilt every winter using fresh ice and snow. Every year, it looks different.

The Tower of Pisa in Italy sank into the soft soil on one side, causing it to lean. To prevent collapse, scientists have given it special supports.

The Great Wall of China was built to keep out invaders. It is so long that it can be seen from space.

The World Trade Center was a group of seven office buildings that opened in New York City in 1973. Two of these buildings were 110-story skyscrapers known as the twin towers—the tallest sights on the New York City skyline. On September 11, 2001, the twin towers and other buildings were destroyed in a terrorist attack.

Index